# SEASON OF TREASON

by Karen Kellock Ph.D.

---

## Manual for Superior Men

A complete theory based on Einstein physics,
Political Psychology, Systems Theory
and Archetypal Psychiatry.

### FORMULA

All success attraction
All disease obstruction
All recovery elimination


You must fast on all three

### OBSTRUCTIONS:

People
Habit
Food

# SEASON OF TREASON

It's the low minds who love to see you suffer. You're a great intellect but they were losers.   Life is a ladder and you were imposed early on by low calibers and this was your lesson/teacher.   Don't relive what low minds did to you when down. Take it as your war: the Fallen Hero Syndrome.   Yes, you were in a jungle of sting-shots and flip-flops, a dystopic depressing social hodgepodge.

# TREASON

You want him to open up to you, walk pastures with you, grow old with you but see reality Sue.

I've been there/done that and know what it's like. Stuck on someone like he's your life?

He's flashy but without true foundation, only a false self which he maintains with every atom.

## GOD SENT A MIRAGE TO TEST

God sent a mirage which you refused cuz you know the scoop then he was cast away like poop.

Narcissists cause incredible stress which makes our reality NARROW. You're missing it all.

The victim sees trouble as outside of her so stops all self-care or questioning her thoughts ever.

His erratic behavior makes us focus only on the narcissist and that's why we get sick.

The left swoops in to create a stink if you commit the crime of wrongthink tho' theirs is rinky dink.

The left always excommunicates its own when they fail to talk orthodoxy, the national foe.

Simply see the art of detaching as a science. Check level of toxicity then reconnect to the nice.

## RID OF TOXIC PEOPLE = ENERGY

When rid of toxic people you'll walk faster, feeling more energy and fascination with life generally.

# TREASON

You long to tell him things but honey he's not listening. He's a narcissist and only into his own thing.

Narc relationships are meant to BREAK you. This is classical and most importantly, spiritual.

Break you: that's why you feel humiliated, exhausted, worthless and often jealous as a fool.

He wants you down and controllable but due to lack of empathy can go too far--that's your exit gal.

**LIMERENCE**

Cycles of abuse between intermittent reinforcement creates high emotions = LIMERENCE.

The highs and lows of an abusive relationship creates high chemical action and then limerence.

The mix of abuse and gifts creates trauma bonds and it's all chemical reaction to contradiction.

The highs and lows of abusive relationship seem like love and excitement but its never worth it.

Since it comes from other people, mental illness is prevented by BOUNDARIES against evil.

Reduce that person's access to you. Reduce contact by deleting options--now you'll be well Sue.

Don't feel guilty for outgrowing people who had the chance to grow with you but stayed evil.

You shouldn't be thinking of him/her at all. YOU'RE the goldmine but destiny is blocked if you fall.

You're have a fantasmagoria to focus on were you not so tunnel-visioned on a futile infatuation.

# TREASON

It was the chemistry of hopes vs. disappointments which was the catalyst to cling to this fling.

Sickened by constant disappointments you say HIM as the solution and kept spreading your net.

It's all about REALITY which can change in an instant as we switch tunnel vision to the ultimate.

Sickened by constant disappointments you saw HIM as the solution and kept spreading your net.

I hereby go cold turkey on my chemical reactions to contradiction. That old life was sick son.

## FRAILTY OF MORALS

His body was strong but his morals were frail. Due to this frailty our home was a grenade range see.

When you finally see it's his empty lack of input that keeps you hooked you'll be shocked.

Coming back to SELF is a fabulous shock, a psychic opening to glory. See him again: no, sorry.

See him again, you'd rather have the Self–like when you eat again you'd rather have the fast.

There's nothing like that day you re-discovered Self, and you recall that to avoid the narc hell.

The day I re-discovered Self after narc hell I was so jubilant I walked all day amidst flower smells.

After experiencing your right brain cornucopia after a dark tunnel, going back won't interest ya.

I wanna stay whole and happy now. I've even lost weight as things are flowing again, wow.

# TREASON QUEENS

SUDDEN REVERSALS AND GHOSTING
WE MUST GHOST THE NARCISSIST
HE'S ENTITLED TO TRAMPLE
EXPECT REVENGE WHEN YOU DISENGAGE
SOUL TIES ARE SEXUAL
A HAUNTED HOUSE OF BROKEN DREAMS
WHAT DID I SAY OR DO?
WHAT IS A WISE WOMAN?
ENTERTAINING INFERIORS
LIFE IS TOUGH GROWING UP
HE LONGS FOR THAT CONVERSATION
EASY TO START, HARD TO END
A WALKING BALL OF CONFUSION
SOUL TIES TO PORN STARS
ANOSOGNOSIA
THE CRAVING TO CORRECT
MUST DEPRIVE THE FLESH
GRANDIOSE NARCISSISM
DETACHED TRICKSTER
TYRANNICAL [MALIGNANT] NARCISSISM
MY SELFIX ROUTINES
MADWOMAN TO THEORETICIAN

# TREASON QUEENS

The feeling of going beyond a problem or a project accomplished is so delicious I'm lovin' it.

Why should invaders determine your day? You plan every inch of it, interruptions keep away.

On our enlightening spiritual journey we wake up to all forms of abuse while before we were obtuse.

At first, they never met anyone as great as you. Over time, they ghost you and even eschew.

## SUDDEN REVERSALS AND GHOSTING

Ghosting is a form of dominance and control. One grows crazy [what is goin' on?] and old.

Ghosting is abruptly ending all communication with someone without an explanation.

Suffering and pain: Manipulations, gaslighting, bullying, triangulations and smear campaigns.

As all three systems are full throttle--attachment, need to please, inner critic--she falls off pedestal.

What are they, emotional vampires? YES. They feed off your emotional stress as they create chaos.

While we just improve the work and live rationally, they plot and plan how to ruin us suddenly.

Why does therapy fail for a narcissist? They won't be accountable and they won't self-reflect.

When walking away we don't write an explanation just hold our heads high on the way out, amen.

# TREASON QUEENS

We've spent a lifetime explaining ourselves to these types and so now we don't do this, aye.

I felt punished for decades until I finally woke up and put up boundaries and now it's a party daily.

Ghosting is for our emotional wellness and peace of mind. Flip-flops are his thing but we wanna be high.

## WE MUST GHOST THE NARCISSIST

Now we choose to ghost and ignore the narcissist. It's not revenge it's safety and healing first.

Psychologically unstable or violent relationships can be gossip alone and we must escape quick.

When we reach the end of our rope we may simply stop talking/wasting our breath and good energy.

We ghost the narcissist just like that. We don't lurk on his pages or fantasize and we don't look back.

You'll feel so much better honey without this fickle fiend who makes you crazy, even intentionally.

Ghost him. He's not your friend and God doesn't want you hanging with such unstable fickle men.

We cannot unsee the horrifying nightmare we've already experienced. We're hep now sis.

The only way we can go back now is to become mentally ill again like thru drinking or hitting bottom.

There will be no more arguing or giving away our precious energy. All our minutes go for destiny.

This is going to fire up the narcissist and any other spiteful, hateful, toxic person who's sick.

# TREASON QUEENS

They will be ENRAGED so expect the unexpected sister. Remember, we did not write a letter.

Rage reactions: infantile or adolescent tantrums and retaliations. Hoover apologies: maudlin.

How dare you have healthy boundaries, how dare you not let me control you/make you crazy.

## HE'S ENTITLED TO TRAMPLE

The narc feels entitled to trample all your boundaries. Remember this at all times, please honey.

Scorned and mocked: maybe it's time we stop hiding from this and instead stay away/put stops.

YES they actually feel entitled to hurt you over, and over and over again, with no accountability amen.

They feel entitled to smear you name all over the place and since they're family it's credible disgrace.

They're entitled to destroy you, resettle you, annihilate you--taking the kids, pets and house too.

They want to violate you and to hurt you badly. This is not for kiddies, it's mad max like in cities.

Don't assume or count on a thing from them or be left hanging. Love God then do your own thing.

Since it's about their entitlement they will seek revenge. Get restraining orders, relocate, get a fence.

## EXPECT REVENGE WHEN YOU DISENGAGE

You need to stay safe and keep your kids/pets away cuz nothing's off limits to this rage-filled guy.

# TREASON QUEENS

They will triangulate with every possible person they can, making them all see you as a madman.

This is what they crave. They love to stir the pot then looking back at the devastation, amazed.

Now it's crystal clear who are for you and who are against you so now at least you know.

Going no-contact preserves your mental health, stability, security and sense of sanity.

Why explain to them when they don't care. Conserve your energy to stay optimal now my dear.

If they refuse to take responsibility for their actions, why keep talkin'? It's fruitless, benefitting no one.

The narcissist will kill your pets. Nothing's off limits when getting back at you, the resistants.

Even after relocation I fear them coming around the corner. It's a trauma dealing with invaders.

Years of chronic narcissistic abuse linked to chronic pain, PTSD, anxiety, depression and addiction.

## SOUL TIES ARE SEXUAL

How easily we're unequally yoked and then bound through sex as if with a rope to a loser or dope.

How easily we slip into soul ties where all you're thinking about is that girl or guy. Sex is powerful, aye.

Lovebombing is also irrational, hyper-flattery. Wait for the change sure to come quite quickly.

The attachment is activated, you have no idea why you're being ghosted: this is the gist.

# TREASON QUEENS

You're insecure and anxious but that's what they want: to take something precious and mess it up.

You're pushed into a position to worry about what they think, drastically lowering self-esteem.

It's a division you'll have to agree on: "It's not that my husband is ghosting me, I just never see him".

Is it that they reverse, or you found out fast? Don't get too close at first, chaperones are a MUST.

## A HAUNTED HOUSE OF BROKEN DREAMS

Most moderns are haunted houses of broken dreams and relationships: in short, they're twits.

Since the whole point is REVERSALS, relationships take much time and patience being watchful.

A queen must have her own life strategy and source of income to not depend on a man, firstly.

You didn't say it the way they wanted you to say it so now they're ignoring you: the human race.

What I went through before knowing these truths as propounded here brought a hellish fear.

## WHAT DID I SAY OR DO?

She's left wondering: what did I say, what did I do? Seeing symbols of deep meaning--paranoid shrew.

Never forget a narcissist will stop at nothing to reach the top quickly, he'll sacrifice you honey.

He throws you off balance "you always think the worst of people", you're oversensitive and a bitch.

# TREASON QUEENS

Adult children of alcoholics guess at what normal is. Inappropriate things they know not to resist.

Here's his scenario: I got you, I pulled you up then I pushed you off the pedestal by ghosting you.

They know you're weak if you investigate why you've been erased, then they persecute you ok.

They can unleash their wrath on you--the softhearted-- and say whatever they want, so don't do it.

Stop trying to figure him cuz he's not rational/just wants to create instability in you, the emotional.

He did it to push your boundaries, make you feel insecure and test your tolerance for sure.

## WHAT IS A WISE WOMAN?

A throne is a terrible thing to waste so make haste in getting rid of this guy and the latter day haze.

For a wise woman getting in touch with herself is more important than connections to others.

The wife-women come across as odd or strange to the ordinary liberal mind which is so deranged.

To most women self-discovery is foreign--they're raised up to be with a man and that's all hon'.

A broken queen pursues one man after another whereas the wise one's into self-discovery forever.

Without a firm handle on herself she allows others into her life, heart, head and bed: used up.

## ENTERTAINING INFERIORS

# TREASON QUEENS

The unconscious queen doesn't realize the throne in the room is hers so she entertains inferiors.

She never learned/was never taught that getting in touch with self is the most important.

Your "type" of man rarely turns out to be your husband as "type" refers mostly to sexual attraction.

Wake up and you'll kick yourself for being with bums who didn't even deserve a conversation.

She developed full blown soul ties with people because she didn't know who she was for real.

You can ACT a part all you want ala Shakespeare but without moral curbs it's still all inferior.

Living in the land of liberal La La/dumb was no fun: my Ph.D. in the streets-- Satan's kingdom.

Women didn't want you influencing their kids and men invaded like magnets/just wanted sex.

## LIFE IS TOUGH GROWING UP

Life was tough growing up. She couldn't trust females and hardly ever males: the Odd Girl Out.

If I teamed with females I always did 90%, if I trusted them I always wished to hell I hadn't.

It's not how they're born, it's how feminism & lack of instruction has made em, and it's masculine.

Gotta be ready to catch the thought/take a vain imagination captive along with lies ya' bought.

It begins with heartbreak that invites others in for solace but then it all spirals down and it's hellish.

# TREASON QUEENS

All that happened to make you tough, to build social muscle, to ignore it/let it fall off as fluff.

Just like Lucas ragingly like a madman defends Mark in *The Rifleman*, that's your Papa in Heaven.

The main problem with the narcissist is fickleness: love then discard can even cause psychosis.

"Your wife doesn't know what she has" while a soul tie is being stirred up along with his pride.

## HE LONGS FOR THAT CONVERSATION

He begins to long for that conversation, he calls her for no reason, at night he's thinkin//dreamin'.

It leads to a broken family with kids, pets and a house, emotionally unavailable to your spouse.

She can't stand being touched since body's with him but mind's on the other side of town again.

The hidden cost of soul ties is enormous and ruinous but minimized while in the mental circus.

The biggest way enemy seeks to bind us/control us is illicit relationships: thrilling bur ruinous.

Soul ties pull you back into the bondage of Egypt. Always pulling you back tho' you reject it.

## EASY TO START, HARD TO END

It's very easy to develop soul ties but it can cost you the rest of your life: the evil bands are tight.

For a man or woman of purpose, the soul tie robs them of energy and as for God it pulls em away.

# TREASON QUEENS

With a soul tie all you do is think about him. You can't be creative/God can't get thru the fog hon'.

With a soul tie you can't forgive yourself. God has but you're distracted, constantly living in hell.

Everything you see in the world is viewed against the backdrop of HIM. It is mental enslavement.

Feeling unworthy of absolutely anything and everything, a soul tie can rob you of healthy living.

What are the implications of sexual treachery? It's the confusion between spirit, mind and body

## A WALKING BALL OF CONFUSION

She was a walking ball of confusion as he pushed the limits of perversion for a soul tie foundation.

The big impact of a soul tie is doing something wrong that you hate, keeping you from being great.

You go down wrong street, you buy the wrong thing--it's all from confusion and soul ties see.

A soul tie consumes consciousness in fear of relapse but that just creates a lifeline to illicit sex.

A soul tie creeps in/reconfigures subconscious mind. She can't pull away, reprogrammed by Satan.

The enemy works subconsciously to pull you back before you know where you are in fact.

Why did he wake up with a witch? The settings of his soul underneath had been tampered with.

When a man pushes her sexual limits he's reprogramming her soul--she even gets brazen/bold.

# TREASON QUEENS

She was the same woman devoted to God but having been reprogrammed, she's now just a slut.

Why keep going there? Her subconscious awareness has been skewered, she's no longer rare.

A soul tie can develop just by seeing a porn queen on the screen. She's now knit to your soul see.

Perverted data became ignited planting seeds in you so now you can't have a relationship of just two.

## SOUL TIES TO PORN STARS

Having soul ties to porn stars & people/grudges from his past he can't have intimacy with spouse.

He's pushed to have multiple experiences, now one woman can't fulfill him even with substances.

He may love his wife but longs for the things the manifold spirits lodged in his heart see.

As a soul tie reprograms the mind there are deficiencies created then longing for the same kind.

The deficiency reveals itself in craving bad things to compensate, and so the cycle repeats ok.

It creates a deficiency of vital necessities while bringing on a craving for the things that destroy see.

As it develops the soul tie turns off prioritization of God and growth and it's like a mind's been sold.

## ANOSOGNOSIA

Craving things that will kill you is anosognosia, the major blind spot of all addictions in America.

# TREASON QUEENS

Soul ties drive some into a cave of emotional unavailability: its you their eyes can't see.

Tho' the tie's broken and the longing forsaken you're still not emotionally available for a new one.

God ordained you queen so despite a sexual past so embarrassing you still gotta do your thing.

## THE CRAVING TO CORRECT

He took advantage of your craving to correct a past situation, to be loved, to have attachment.

He kept pushing her sexual limits to implant roots of a soul die deeper in, to make her a fool again.

Painful memories despite a peaceful present will cause even queens to forfeit their throne I said.

Painful memories of doing something you didn't want to all due to that soul tie better eschewed.

Soul ties drive you into a cave and make you emotionally blank to those trying to help but can't.

## MUST DEPRIVE THE FLESH

The biggest problem of ridding soul ties is depriving the flesh. No instant answers, just no sex.

You don't want to but you must: deprive flesh while building up spirit by discipline/resistance.

You must develop a new respect for God's word which is a quick and powerful, two-edged sword.

The word of God reveals the intents of the heart: our hidden motives, flushed out at the start.

# TREASON QUEENS

The subconscious reprogramming of the soul creeps in unawares then our motives get vile/unfair.

It's the influence of demonic forces on your mind and flesh, that's why it's so hard to resist.

One cannot break soul ties without the power of the holy spirit. Prayer, no contact/sex will do it.

If the soul tie partner lives with you, stay calm but pray God for a separation for this is wrong too.

He's doing nothing for your life but incarcerating a vision and destiny so return to decency/be free.

## GRANDIOSE NARCISSISM

The grandiose need for admiration comes from feeling worthless and being of no consequence.

Due to fear they get desperate: putting their best image forward of themselves, a raison d'être.

The fear of being inconsequential and insignificant is so great they compensate every day.

To keep at bay any negative perceptions he turns on the charm but when not needed turns it down.

He over-inflates his achievements, even outright lies about degrees, awards, sexual conquests.

The image is: he's superior and got it together. Above all he loves triggering envy in others.

He is trying to prove not just to others but himself that he is superior and workaholism is near.

They will devalue or dismiss people who don't share their agenda or image of themselves.

# TREASON QUEENS

Giving accolades at first but then jealousy erupts and he feels one-upped, down in the dumps.

This is where Hitler types murder those who brought them to power: jealousy is triggered.

They are great, without defect or fault. The slightest disagreement with this and they will erupt.

Not believing the cool-aid they've been drinking about themselves, they hit a conflict and mess.

We see explosion of shameless self-promotion in social media--a hotbed of narcissistic pathology.

He reaches a fork in the road: either believe his deception or face reality that he's a toad.

In great diminishment he sees the gross exaggeration he's portrayed--worse it was public too ok.

If he accepts he over-sold himself he goes through psychological regression to a sinister hell.

He will face depression then ground himself in something holistic/real [vs. the old narcissism].

## DETACHED TRICKSTER

At the second level the narc can't go back to inferior so he becomes a pro: the detached trickster.

Inferiority is lost to their conscious mind and they're deeply committed to manipulating for supply.

They're committed now and the world is their stage. The ego and public persona are one ok.

He moves from the need for admiration to the need for advantage and he rules without conscience.

# TREASON QUEENS

They've fully integrated in an unhealthy way the superior image--no more room for insecurity/shame.

They've fully integrated a superior image in an unhealthy way--no more room for insecurity/shame.

Their sense of superiority or brilliance gives them entitlement to exploit/take advantage.

At this level a need for advantage turns to deception and trickery cuz it's about supply, shamelessly.

They've so sold out to their grandiose image it's become their god and the end of this is not good.

The grandiose, superior image must win at all costs having lost heart connection to all else.

## TYRANNICAL [MALIGNANT] NARCISSISM

At this level it's no more "am I really that great?" because now it's locked and loaded ok.

It's very difficult because of the defenses that are operating to go back, causing panic attacks.

He is unapologetic at this point: people are SUPPLY-- devalued, banished and discarded, aye.

At this point he's gained so much success cheatin', selling out the ego to traits like plagiarism.

"Malignant narcissism is the precursor to psychopathy" they say but let's just call it grandiosity.

Fraud, plagiarism, lying on a resume are the biggest signs of the grandiose narcissist today.

Expect high levels of aggression when seeking dominance: careful cuz it can lead to violence.

# TREASON QUEENS

Using deception by any means to come out the winner on top is dangerous in divorce courts.

On the next level of psychopathic bully the narc has reached immense success so stays a sadist.

Tyrannical: at this point he takes great pleasure in seeing people uncomfortable or miserable.

Gaining pleasure at hurt shows the total loss of narcissistic conscience marking this jerk.

Extreme paranoia is common at this level if the individual sees his empire begin to topple.

## MY SELFIX ROUTINES

Music listening is the most thrilling part of the day. I take it seriously & leave time for it ok.

Fasting levels the playing field. Any dumbass ugly joker can do it and become a prince healed.

Food will not fill that hole and you're never hungry anyway: why not fast/BECOME whole.

We eat to not remember. Why not not-eat to face the memory and dissolve it forever and ever?

## MADWOMAN TO THEORETICIAN

The young genius doesn't have time for social niceties so shows the primitive archetype you see.

I'll admit I was a madwoman who didn't ever know what she was doin' and felt entitled to it even.

The work is done, the empire has been built, the theory's been written and I'm here still.

# TREASON QUEENS

The theoretician states the paradigm and formula, the techs follow with specific proofs for ya.

You did the Great Work and Wonder with your own two hands, you deserve acclaim/remuneration.

You battled ridicule, disdain and censorship all your life, a giant sacrifice-- banishment and misery.

It took fifty years to make it look easy. To state the case that y'all know underneath anyway.

The theoretician-discoverer has rare energy to be able to accomplish this, the New Paradigm.

Being modern is catching the eternal in the transitory, something that's far bigger than us you see.

# QUEENS AND TREASON

LET GO OF INHERITED SHAME
FEMALE SELF-CONCEPT SHRINK: SEX
PERVERSION OF ESLF-IDENTITY
BATTERED TARGET: EXTERNAL FORCES
WOMEN:  TOO EMOTIONAL FOR SUCCESS
SUBTRACTING FROM GOD'S POWER
POWERFUL WOMEN DEALING WITH MEN
CREEPING INTO WOMEN'S HOUSES
COMMUNIST SPIRIT
BEING. DIFFERENT AND DIVA STATUS
POWER WOMEN VALUE FINANCIAL INDEPENDENCE
POWER WOMEN SELF-ACTUALIZE
INSECURITY LOWERS POTENTIAL
SUPERIOR FEMALES PRODUCE RESULTS FAST
STUDY HOW MEN THINK AND PROGRESS
THINK BEFORE YOU TALK
GRUDGES ARE ANCHORS TO BAD PAST
POWER WOMEN DRESS LIKE IT
POWER WOMEN WATCH THEIR WORDS
POWER WOMEN NURTURE SEEDS OF GREATNESS
POWER WOMEN LOVE GOD FIRST
TRAUMA BONDING
TRAUMA IN THE WOMB/BORN EVIL
NAÏVE TRANSMITTERS OF MOM'S ANGER
NARCISSISTS CHOOSE THE VULNERABLE
THE SPIRIT MADE A HOME IN YOU
NARC VICTIMS ARE ATTACKED AGAIN
NOT A NARC MAGNET JUST A MAGGOT TOLERANT
IF THEY TREATED MOM LIKE THAT...
HAPPY RAINBOW BECAME A BLACK CLOUD
JESUS SAID LET DEAD BURY DEAD
THEY WANT YOUR MELTDOWN
LOVING HER HURTING
HIX POLITIX RUMINATIONS
RECAP ON DAILY ROUTINES

# QUEENS AND TREASON

**LET GO OF INHERITED SHAME**

Let go of the inherited shame, people's games or how sick you became: get a fresh start today.

If you've been in just one codependent or dysfunctional relationship it acts as a relational template.

I realized suddenly I was exhilaratingly happy when alone and miserable in the social world.

It was such a damper on my happy reality as I felt my spirit sucked right outa me. I was 23.

How to outsmart the narcissist blocking God's kingdom: get wisdom on the signs and symptoms.

No more will you fuel the fires of narcissistic supply. No more overridden or ignored by that guy.

As if it wasn't enough going through it that one time it compels you to do it again/cross the line.

All hell happens when the devil knocks and you let him in. Practice saying "NO": do it now friend.

The end of debate: If you're not in lockstep you're dead, blackballed, ostracized, bad rep.

Most important point in psychology: trauma can bring a collapse of morals and boundaries.

They have a family: they have each other, while you're the lone ranger always feeling an outsider.

**FEMALE SELF-CONCEPT SHRINK: SEX**

# QUEENS AND TREASON

Instead of recognizing you for accomplishments the lowminds are jealous laying on their couches.

A queen emboldens her husband with undistracted purpose and relentless pursuit of her vision.

Power women have the character, determination and intellect to produce despite circumstance.

Woman has power to dominate as a man but society diminishes self-concept before she can.

If society sees her as a mere sex object she'll begin to project sexuality over intellect any day.

She goes into her Ph.D. orals exam projecting sexuality: such is the mixup caused by warped society.

She projects her sexuality over spirituality in "accepted" perversion as society morally slides down.

"You wanna get naked?" Inwardly she cringes but in fear of ridicule goes along tho' shaken.

It is SO ridiculous she doesn't know how to answer it so in shamed resolution bites the bullet.

Nakedness is symbolic of a distorted self-view--when sexuality's used as a success strategy too.

When a woman sleeps around the enemy's perverted her identity & she's swept along mindlessly.

Of course men want sex but she doesn't seem to know that, giving into the base desires of brats.

## PERVERSION OF ESLF-IDENTITY

So let's take this as our starting point: Today, women's identity is perverted so God can't anoint.

# QUEENS AND TREASON

In conforming to social expectations she's just a sex symbol triggering many early assaults.

A sex receptacle or baby maker. If it's how she's viewed she'll adapt by being fat or a starver.

Romans 12: 2: Don't be conformed to this [dirty] world but transformed by renewing your mind.

To conform means to SQUEEZE something into shape from the outside. The world attacks you ok.

The world attacks you in the form of hatred sensed on every level but conformity makes it stable.

A nonconforming female is called an Inconvenient Woman and she'd better be strong man.

## BATTERED TARGET: EXTERNAL FORCES

They were rough on you. The unintelligent don't have the finesse/restraint but they forget it too.

She's a battered target from external forces: not only media but fans of that view coming at ya.

Ignorant religion, messages in music, misjudgments in critics, can't find rubies only lunatics.

Being squeezed into a form--Procrustean conformity--strips her of queen power instantly.

To kill the storm powerful females conquer emotions, not a rollercoaster like most women.

Female emotional flip floppers are unpredictable and live lives of instability. Early on, that was me.

If a woman is to be respected she must conquer her emotions like the alpha male/old fashioned.

# QUEENS AND TREASON

Give into your emotions and you'll never be respected as a powerful woman, so do this now.

## WOMEN:  TOO EMOTIONAL FOR SUCCESS

The first thing the world says: women are too emotional for serious responsibility and it's obvious.

An intrusive thought triggers day-long crying mania. This is introversion reversed, female hysteria.

I cried an ocean of tears & finally matured. Tears on my pillow for years calling on the Lord.

Triple Pisces I guess, the path was paved with tears. Driven into total solitude from the herd.

Now I'm all cried out & well fortified. Nothing surprises me but a fence and locked gate helps see.

Relationally I'd swing from strange unexplained loves and hatreds to a target, being boundariless.

In a woman-hating world she slips into whatever works: sex. Without even realizing it she's a slut.

A woman as president? "Can we trust a woman with the button?" We all know the sudden bedlam.

A woman can't do X, Y and Z cuz she's too emotional, that's what the world says to us all.

Too emotional: He who has no rule over his own spirit is like a city broken down without walls.

## SUBTRACTING FROM GOD'S POWER

An emotional woman subtracts from the power God gave her to walk in. Use your brain.

# QUEENS AND TREASON

I did thoughtless things before I matured but you forgive yourself then just continue to endure.

Older spouse: I realized he was not mature he was an alcoholic, that age had little to do with it.

If a woman doesn't have control of her own emotions, someone else will manipulate her soul.

Thinking it's ok to have emotional breakdowns in public: girls gotta act like dudes not lunatics.

You are a leader, a queen in your own right. So you gotta be respected and not cry like that.

Leaders are not out of control emotionally: always maudlin or angry, going off on people daily.

She can't have her feelings hurt over every little thing. She's gotta man up, that's being a queen.

Consciously establish your own emotional expectations: stop letting em push your buttons.

## POWERFUL WOMEN DEALING WITH MEN

Can you go into environments where there are haters and still maintain emotional balance?

Establish emotional expectations: if they do this I will do that--practice being under the gun.

Study women who thrive in high pressure environments. You may not like Oprah but that's power man.

The queen uproots strongholds: of self-doubt, insecurity and lack of assertion/being bold.

The queen self-correct immediately when emotions start to surge. She nips em in the bud first.

# QUEENS AND TREASON

Powerful women are students of how men think. No entering lion's cage without studying em see.

A queen studies men's tricks so society can't take advantage, trip her up or make her sick.

She learns from men who love her unconditionally: fathers, brothers, pastors show her fatherly.

Would-be queens like men who break em down/destroy em emotionally and wreck their self-esteem.

She can't study a man's mind if she's talking all the time. Most women can't be silent, aye.

A fool uttereth his mind but the wise keeps silent until after: that's insight to the male mentality sir.

Pay attention to what a man doesn't say as much as he does say--not a vacuous blabbermouth ok.

I'm not part of any community: I don't want em telling me how to do things or what to eat.

## CREEPING INTO WOMEN'S HOUSES

No you can't come over again! Why do you think I'm out here? If I were social I'd be in town.

The world tries to debase a woman. This undertow can come thru a housekeeper or the mailman.

She came over with a friend I didn't even know and started railing at me--in my own home!

This severe undertow in the world is overcome by superior females, teaching boys/girls.

You tried getting out of it with that creepy clown but he managed to talk you back into it again.

## COMMUNIST SPIRIT

Communist spirit is taking over where people are afraid to say anything or show their things.

What I learned in a tiny cabin: it wasn't about a mansion but my own SPACE alone.

But did it give me solitude? It attracted em like flies, they too wanted escape from the rude.

So I had to draw lines--it's "just me out here". They took that as rejection: invasive intruders.

They wanted to hang out in my cabin to share the solitude in nature. I was forlorned dear.

The reason it hurt so much is cuz people are cruel and crude not cuz you're a bad person dude.

Most men don't listen to their wives or any other woman so be very grateful if you found one.

Pornography: being impotent from prostate and aneurysms in head he used it as therapy.

## BEING. DIFFERENT AND DIVA STATUS

Even in my non-sinning prepubescence people sensed my differences and I agonized over this.

There is prejudice regarding skin color, race, culture, gender but also just being DIFFERENT.

Sensing non-verbal rejection they look for solace and there starts a crutch, an addiction--sin.

Then the rejection becomes STIGMA--a nut job, a fool--then the group all chimes in to be cool.

# QUEENS AND TREASON

She found out I apologized to her knowing she was wrong as her pride went upside down.

Powerful women study men. Most women don't but men sure study them to push buttons.

Avoid diva status--with a closet full of clothes but a bank account full of nothing/overdrafts.

You're a diva with money in the bank and non-dependence, not with clothes in your closet.

## POWER WOMEN VALUE FINANCIAL INDEPENDENCE

Powerful women value financial independence. Poverty is a women's issue and many are homeless.

Wisdom is a defense even as money is a defense. You've gotta get some money and fast.

A woman's greatest need is security. Money is that but if she disrespects it it'll be gone see.

Powerful women have a healthy relationship with making, managing and multiplying money.

Start managing money in your own right and you won't be going after more broke dudes, aye.

A wise woman prepares to handle financial issues cuz she never knows what the future holds.

It's much better to have a Mercedes in the bank than one in the driveway. Pastor Blakes

It dishonors God to honor relationships [seeking marriage] not full potential development.

## POWER WOMEN SELF-ACTUALIZE

# QUEENS AND TREASON

Powerful women self-actualize: they maximize their full potential--what future husbands recognize.

Number 1: Powerful women are happy with themselves and make great mates for great men.

A great/superior woman is not into impressing people but becoming an impressive person.

Avoid relationships that divorce you from yourself. You can't self-actualize in that matrix of hell.

Powerful women don't tolerate insecurity within themselves knowing how it affects all of us.

## INSECURITY LOWERS POTENTIAL

Insecurity: a mindset making you behave beneath potential--even flattering people beneath you.

Sucking up to people beneath you brings disrespect cuz with low self-esteem all animals sense it.

Behaving beneath your potential brings even more insecurity and sucking up to the low.

Being subordinate to people beneath you is your season of treason/learning how to survive too.

When insecure those beneath you will start to manipulate, completing your fall from great.

A queen knows nobody else can fit her crown. If a pastor's wife, no worries about other women.

If so filled with insecurities you don't need a man yet. Stay home and let the Lord work on it.

We are self-limiters. We fear other people's opinions but God said be not afraid of their faces.

# QUEENS AND TREASON

Having success in this life is being sure and confident that you are IT. Number one, smart/fit.

Insecurity likes social comfort zones so into uncomfortable positions it must be forced.

Insecurity will never leave quietly. It must be forced out by analyzing everything she's thinking.

Insecurity lives in the dark of internalization. Excuses must be called out by it's carrier, the person.

## SUPERIOR FEMALES PRODUCE RESULTS FAST

A superior woman has the character, strength and intellect to produce life results fast.

You busted my boundaries/brought an army after I said I wanted privacy so I wanna be alone see.

Regardless of obstacles and circumstances the superior female lives with undistracted purpose.

Relentless pursuit of personal vision marks great women who can't be bumped off course by man.

She is not stopped by anything or anyone. There is nothing that breaks her in that vision.

She will break through any obstacle to get where God predestined for her and it's like a miracle.

If not in control of emotions, someone else is. You're not ready for responsibility the world says.

I thought I had the right to be an emotional basket case but from this disgrace I fell from grace.

## STUDY HOW MEN THINK AND PROGRESS

# QUEENS AND TREASON

A superior female studies how men think. No going into the lion's den without studying it see.

When he resumed drinking career after three years the hedge was down and in came the herd.

I don't want God mad at me again. Caution: stay in line for His punishments are brutal man.

Only new age idiots think He's an all-loving God. He hates iniquity & rewards when we're good.

## THINK BEFORE YOU TALK

You must be very careful in life to stay in line. I took so many chances going out alone at night.

Don't say wild outlandish things you'll have to eat later. Note: everything is recorded/beware.

Be yourself in boardroom or playing with dogs. Be comfortable with men/I repeat: be yourself.

She studies a male-dominated perverted society where men are in control and see women as prey.

Powerful women have money in the bank not on their backs--they aren't waiting for Mr. Flash.

Superior females focus on self-actualization, not wishin'/hopin' for a man to come around.

Great women manifest themselves, not waiting for wedding bells but Kings find em after all.

## GRUDGES ARE ANCHORS TO BAD PAST

No more bitterness. Power women dispose of the trash in pursuit of the treasure: being highness.

# QUEENS AND TREASON

What holds a woman down in mediocrity is bitterness: holding onto grudges, arguing with ghosts.

Holding onto stuff, drinking the poison and wanting their death. Woman, you gotta empty the trash.

You gotta forgive and move on. Men duke it out then become chums, women hold grudges in.

Bitterness is for small people but female greatness is from regular spiritual detox/clarity too.

You gotta let it go girl. You mad at a guy you knew 30 years ago but he's a grandpa now ya know?

A grudge is an anchor locking you to part of your past you should wanna forget about at last.

The culprit forgot about you long ago but a grudge makes him huge in your mind, all aglow.

Like spoiled food odors throughout, holding trash in your heart disrupts the entire environment.

## POWER WOMEN DRESS LIKE IT

Powerful women dress intentionally. Play the part to be seen as a leader taken seriously,

Tho' it's good to be a looker you can't dress like a hooker and attract a good husband/earner.

You can't dress like you came off the pole and think you'll be offered a seat in a boardroom girl.

Sleazy dress locks you out of the circle God intends for you to walk in. Dress chic, nothin' sparkling.

It doesn't matter how educated or shrewd, if you don't dress right no one pays attention to you.

# QUEENS AND TREASON

The best woman in the world misrepresented herself thru dress code which is her billboard young/old.

Not only dressing loosely and slutty but not put together entirely: wearing slippers to town or city.

Not spending all your money on shoes or clothes but putting your stuff together--it all goes.

If you don't dress like someone's wife your husband will never recognize you. Grow up not "cool".

The world only sees what we project and responds according to our signals: think about that.

God looks at the heart but man the outward appearance, not the intellect or spirit first.

You can't be too loose or sloppy but dress like the queen you are starting today. A fresh start ok.

## POWER WOMEN WATCH THEIR WORDS

Powerful women never settle for a weak man. Weak women do but they're never happy then.

He's weak without backbone and you're settling. It's never gonna work despite virtue signaling.

Unequally yoked: you dream of reaching the stars but he's satisfied with street lights or bars.

When a woman talks to a man any kind of way it means he's too weak for her/won't last anyway.

Why would she hitch herself to a man who's too weak to lead her? Growth stops/not going anywhere.

Powerful women don't offend in speech, cussin' folk out. They wait for right time to be loud.

# QUEENS AND TREASON

Women cussin' like thugs. Loud, ignorant pugnacity seen on reality shows is what it's about.

She opens her mouth in skillful Godly wisdom, on her tongue the law of kindness [no cussin'].

Giving counsel and instruction in kindness by her highness, not a brash and crude feminist.

A woman can tear her house down with her mouth. Her words break a man down or build him up.

She's uniquely designed to give birth to what's in a man. Words are creative material in the kingdom.

## POWER WOMEN NURTURE SEEDS OF GREATNESS

By using her words properly she can nurture seeds of greatness in a man to be awe-inspiring.

Build him up to his predestined greatness please. Recall: wise women do not offend in speech.

A fool uttereth all his mind but a wise man keeps it in until afterwards. That's the proper avatar.

If everything going through your mind comes outa your mouth you're a foolish woman/shut up.

She "keeps house" by "keeping it real" but it's a madhouse of fear and all are out of keel.

People in this world will hurt you. But when keeping it real goes wrong you will be all alone too.

## POWER WOMEN LOVE GOD FIRST

Lastly, powerful women perfect their relationship with God. Not chasing men/friending the flawed.

# QUEENS AND TREASON

When mother/father forsake you, the Lord takes you up. The only constant in this life is God.

When daughters fall in love with Me I will give them husbands. Seek God's love, no worshipping man.

Favor Is deceitful and beauty is vain but a woman who seeks the Lord shall be praised. Prov 31

You're not designed to be an average chick but the queen, the daughter of the King, so be it.

When royalty runs thru your blood you can't live any old way, you're powerful only being in grace.

## TRAUMA BONDING

Narcissists demand your subjugation and significance. You must give that up sis.

Her worth/self-respect weren't just stolen, they were trampled upon. To this day she's down.

Sin is a rejection of divine order of universe and brings on not synchronicity but desynchrony.

We're living in an age of mass mental illness. Healthy mindedness is rare and we're failing fast.

A girl never loved on as a child interprets being hit-on as a love bomb and is swept up every time.

You can be so happy and someone starts picking on you. From light to dark/mood turns blue.

He has a unique position of authority over people who aren't in a good place and takes advantage.

## TRAUMA IN THE WOMB/BORN EVIL

# QUEENS AND TREASON

Are some born evil? Yes if the pregnant mother was angry that spirit passes through people.

You're spiritually traumatized in the womb if she's drinking or angry like in the bedroom.

It's not them the person but a spirit making a home in them. Much of it started being angry at mom.

They hate the mother with her anger passed to them. They yearn for the father who's left em.

Dealing with life via mom's anger means frustration because emotions rule like an angry female.

Children of anger degrade to fear, doubt, insecurity, suicidal thoughts, depression, overeating.

The saints have such a stinging conscience it drives them into isolation just to keep balance.

## NAÏVE TRANSMITTERS OF MOM'S ANGER

They were always drunk/no upbringing. Had to learn the hard way: a fish swimming upstream, drowning.

Mom was always angry, in cycles. Once a week there'd be a brawl about the other past episodes.

You don't know the world but are living thru the mother's anger, a defective biocomputer.

Living thru mother's anger: an emotional basket case with short fuse and throws tantrums too.

A man living thru mom's anger is filled with emotion and frustration like angry females we've known.

Words of narcissist victims: "To this day I suffer with self-doubt and profound grief."

# QUEENS AND TREASON

"I feel like damaged goods. Will I ever be acceptable or lovable?" That's what women feel above all.

I had to get away from the toxic fumes and felt terrified, bewildered, sick at heart, empty.

The point is not to prove something/settle grudges with em but to get as far as you can/above em.

Blocked fame is fear of ridicule: of being attacked or called names, of more smear campaigns.

## NARCISSISTS CHOOSE THE VULNERABLE

The narcissist chooses the vulnerable to get supply so teach victims to outsmart them/not cry.

To make the victim more vulnerable they gaslight constantly: blaming, shaming, guilting.

Who are the ones he grooms and preys upon? Abuse and trauma survivors who feel well now.

He will target the highly sensitive person. That was me and he had a party driving me crazy.

It's the low minds who love to see you suffer. You're a great intellect but they were losers.

Life is a ladder and you were imposed early on by low calibers and this was your lesson/teacher.

For low minds have no finesse--they are not empaths. They are merciless--it hurts recalling the past.

## THE SPIRIT MADE A HOME IN YOU

Born whole, we come into a world that awaits us. Split in two, trashed, chopped up in little pieces.

# QUEENS AND TREASON

When you had the devil in you they responded to "him" not you but the cruelty came to you.

This spirit made a home in you, perhaps from the angry womb and the world responded in kind too.

Angry pregnant mothers who are drugging produces a generation of Satan's entitled minions.

Ironically, the narc will target truthseekers but mostly low income, the weak/disabled/homeless.

He will attack empaths, healers and those who've already suffered narcissistic abuse too.

## NARC VICTIMS ARE ATTACKED AGAIN

There is an extremely high probability a victim of a narcissist will be targeted again sis.

Don't relive what low minds did to you when down. Take it as your war: the Fallen Hero Syndrome.

They seem to know you were the black sheep scapegoat of the family and will target you honey.

Without knowledge a black sheep begins a roller coaster of targetings and life changes suddenly.

Yes, you were in a jungle of sting-shots and flip-flops, a dystopic depressing social hodgepodge.

As a victim of a narcissist you wear a hue and this new guy will hand pick you. Be wise Sue.

It's all about him and you'll be put down and discarded. No matter how he acts today, look forward.

## NOT A NARC MAGNET JUST A MAGGOT TOLERANT

# QUEENS AND TREASON

It's not that you're a narc-magnet but a loss of queen status brought a toleration for maggots.

Broken consciousness increases "tolerance" but reduces exclusivity as the hedge goes away.

Clown doesn't deserve a conversation but here you're kneeling before him, even begging him.

Ok you're alone but that's the superior state. It's lonely at the top but the only way for success ok.

Of all sins the worst was letting people in. To your home, your trust, your confidence, your arms.

It always derailed you from destiny, perhaps taking years away. Go solo, God brings him ok.

People are cruel: when you try to escape you see your terrible fate. Don't get involved/evade.

## IF THEY TREATED MOM LIKE THAT...

If he treated mom like that you wouldn't stand for it but since you don't love YOU he can bring it.

Narcissists target people-pleasers because they are the easiest pushovers: make note of this.

Narcissists gaslight in smear campaigns and lies. That's what they do, nothing changes these guys.

Smeared and gaslit by sisters in her twenties she felt the effects in her 70's: it's their weaponry.

They fabricate rumors, stories and nonsense. Hens going for recognition, inferior intellects.

It's torture living in a world of false accusation cuz we're human--we all wanna feel like loved ones.

# QUEENS AND TREASON

Older sister graduated a liberal university and came back falsely accusing me and I caved see.

## HAPPY RAINBOW BECAME A BLACK CLOUD

Happy rainbow childhood suddenly became a dark cloud. She became aggressive, I felt odd.

False accusation created internal contradiction and an eating disorder emerged: compensation.

When affluent snooty stiff-necked liberals took over our Christian family it was devastating/unhappy.

Family ties disperse the moment we die. We may see em in heaven but earthly "family" is a lie.

It was miserable, the un-family, the lie I was told to buy. These were aliens, I basically detested em.

Around will-reading time evil is flushed out. You see it clearly, something hidden but obvious now.

Jesus said don't even go to their funeral for "who are your sisters? Those who love God."

## JESUS SAID LET DEAD BURY DEAD

Jesus said let the dead bury their dead. The walking dead, zombies/mental illness in the head.

Life is short. Suddenly you're old. You were stuck on the same useless course, no more bold.

There were some I loved, like my father. The others spat all over me spreading vicious lies/rumors.

Most were women, feminists. Tho' virtue signalers they were cruel vindicators and often pissed.

They'd get together in their hen sessions and judicate a matter: how to punish/what to do to her.

They'd ask their neighbors what they thought and they'd give their vicious two cents: hix politix.

They tried to destroy you and triangulate every one of your relationships: a hard fact to accept.

It's mental abuse, bullying and outright cruelty. Sister abuse is a dark, hidden reality see.

They will always pass it off as helping you--gossip called "concern". They pass it along with a smirk.

## THEY WANT YOUR MELTDOWN

At the root of what the narc wants is your meltdown. He wants you crying, totally backed down.

Sister wants you screaming profanities/fighting back. This proves her right, you're a sad sack.

Consider them like savage vampires. They want to suck the life and joy out of you: annihilators.

She pushed my buttons to get an emotional reaction from me: like a prison guard she had me.

We must learn how to starve the narcissist and deprive them of supply: to outsmart them finally.

She sucked life right outa me. For decades I lost voice, was boundaryless, couldn't move/resist.

Tho' one sister died/the other senile in a rest home the effects still last, that's the demonic side.

Outsmart the narc and take back your power. Learn about their tactics and mean spirits.

# QUEENS AND TREASON

The narc thinks he/she knows it all. In a family that means the others conform/take a fall.

They don't want you happy, joyous & celebratory but doom/gloom from their judgmental weaponry.

When she graduated college it was all condemnation and harsh judgements, the end of us.

Gaslighting and malicious remarks spew outa their mouths like butter and you just wanna hit her.

## LOVING HER HURTING

Why do some women desire a man who hurts them? Why are they stuck in such painful bedlam?

Because I'm a woman I'm inferior to him who watches cartoons all day but at least he bill pays.

It's common: what she sees and needs as affection is just him setting up addiction.

The classic situation: she's emotional and genuine but he's calculating with deception.

The relationship morphs into manipulationship but emotional neediness she can't see it.

Your will is subjugated, your judgement circumvented: you are being manipulated.

She's her worst enemy, addicted to the very thing killing her but viewed as friend see.

He grinds you down into a place where you're uncomfortable with anything but it ok.

The victim's so broken she's able to relax in a life-threatening scenario of pain/bad effects.

# QUEENS AND TREASON

He's trying to create a subconscious reality which positions you to never prefer healthy.

By now she's so dysfunctional the only thing she's comfortable with is trauma and drama.

She only desires the man who is hurting her cuz in her mind he's the best she qualifies for.

He's degraded, he's demeaned, he's humiliated but in her bashed state she's still infatuated.

She doesn't feel she deserves a proper relationship/a healthy supportive man: it's a process.

The reason anyone is stuck is due to not feeling in their own mind that they deserve good luck.

Though he's continually hurting her she will never qualify for anything better than this torture.

The lying spirit in man has caused women to settle for abuse and call it normal--have you too?

Family felt like aliens, I didn't know them. When we die these ties vaporize/I'm not a Mormon.

## HIX POLITIX RUMINATIONS

An extremist waves the American flag, the don't tread on me flag or sings the national anthem: bad.

Liberals actually think we conservatives are dangerous and out to kill them and their families sis.

I do love foods/music from other lands/cultures but that doesn't mean I wanna lose my own sir.

Feminist students yelled "you must say he AND she", giant speed bumps to my lecturing capacity.

# QUEENS AND TREASON

Wrinkles are an inside job. it's acid creating em and alkaline removing em-- they "snap" out.

With resistance bands upper arm flab can be tightened up. It's genetic and you want rid of it.

He likes being over there in his "cage" as he calls it and I like being alone here so it works out ok.

Two weeks to live: after grapecure for cancer he looked like a movie star. His wife was floored.

He got well from grapecure but of course they won't give credit--it's from some abstruse element.

The taco revolution vastly simplifies the kitchen scene. Every 1-2 days four tacos/juice or nothing.

## RECAP ON DAILY ROUTINES

Write in the morning and then you're OFF. You gotta unwind from the lowminds and chumps.

I'm everywhere all over the map cuz I'm a theoretician and interested in everything man.

# SEASON OF TREASON

SIN BRINGS HEDGE DOWN
SISTER ABUSE
NARCISSISTIC SIBLING ABUSE IS REAL
SOCIAL RATTLESNAKE IN YOUR CAGE
ENERGY DRAIN OF SELF-DEFENSE
NO CLOSURE JUST PROSPER
ABUSE:  DARK NIGHT OF THE SOUL
I WAS A FOOLISH SYCOPHANT
JESUS CLEARED UP THE WHOLE MESS
IT'S JUST A CHICKEN COOP
JEZEBEL AND FEMALE TRAITORS
IDENTITY & FATAL MENTAL ILLNESS
INTROVERTS, UNITE!
ANGELS AVOID ALCOHOL
SEASON OF TREASON
COLLECTIVE NARCISSISM
HE HATES YOUR AUTONOMY
SMEAR CAMPAIGN
NON-COMPROMISING IS SEXY
DRAWING LINES MAKES EM MAD
THE DECISION TO QUIT
CHEATERS ARE OUT
SUDDEN DEFLATION
YOU FLUSHED EM OUT
STRESSFUL LIVING WITH THE DEVIL
WORLD OF NARCISSISTS AND FREAKS
BIDEN'S BAD. WE'RE BRANDON MAD
BIDEN'S PREJUDICE AGAINST US
IT'S ALL MARXIAN TACTICS
RESENTMENT POLITICS
DEATH OF CITIZENSHIP
SAVIOR OF AMERICA AND THE WEST
CONSERVATIVE MEANS DECENCY

# SEASON OF TREASON

WOMEN HOLD WOMEN DOWN
STRESS SHRINKS THE BRAIN
FEMINISTS LOVE MUSLIMS
AOC A FOOLISH DISGRACE
IMPULSIVE EMERGENCIES OF LEFTIES
FINAL JUSTICE VIA MILITARY TRIBUNALS
BYE BYE NANCY PELOSI
PARTY OF DEATH
IT'S ALL FAKE:  VICTIMIZATION CULTURE
NEW WORLD RICH
FALLEN AMERICAN CHURCHES
KNOW YOUR GENDER: ONE OF TWO
GRADUATE, MARRY, WORK: NO POVERTY
RESPECT UNNECESSARY FOR CRAZY
VIOLENCE NOT PREJUDICE
SINNERS ARE MENTALLY ILL
WE WOMEN KNOW IN OUR BONES
IGNORE IGNORANCE, PUNISH RUDENESS
NEVER STAY STUCK
ELEMENTAL:  LISTEN TO THE WIND
BETRAYAL TRAUMA IS DEEP
SICKLY CYCLICITY
BETRAYAL TRAUMA
RISKING MARRIAGE FOR A NUDE PIC
ISOLATION INCREASES SHATTERING
PORN OBSCURES PERCEPTION OF FEMALES
ECLIPSING REALITY BY HIS INFIDELITY
BARBARIC LATE-TERM ABORTION (DEMS)
SELF-ESTEEM OF OLDER WOMEN SMASHED
WOMEN SELF-CONTRATULATING DOING NOTHING
PSYCHOPATHS IN POLITICS
THE "UNITY" (FAKE) CHRISTIAN ELITE
ACHING GUT TELLS ALL
GREEN HEADACHES

# SEASON OF TREASON

**SIN BRINGS HEDGE DOWN**

When in sin you're in a trash bin. Automatically you attract the dangerous and repel the good son.

You sin and the hedge is down. There's a knock on your door directing your new bad direction.

Stop blaming your attackers and start repenting and God will put the protective hedge back.

Look at them as just Satan's helpers and you'll see them slither away when you're back on top sir.

Don't get caught in the trap of grudge but see it as a natural leak in the boat with sin as such.

Once he took that first drink [resumed his drinking career] Satan's minions were at the door.

**LESS WORDS, MORE POWER.** Shut up. You talk too much. The minute you start they turn off.

Don't blame John or Harry but yourself for sinning again then attracting this present catastrophe.

**SISTER ABUSE**

I spent my whole early life escaping misjudgment. I was anxiety-ridden and I feared the stupid.

You hurt me so much I'd daily cry. You destroyed my reputation and relationship with that guy.

Just cuz Golden Girls did a skit on sister abuse doesn't make it funny. It can be criminal honey.

# SEASON OF TREASON

Just cuz Carol Burnett did comedy skits on sister squabbles doesn't make it more palatable.

Your stumbling block is your stepping stone to good as all the pain is turned around/understood.  .

The Dark Night of the Soul is a period of spiritual transformation not just pain/humiliation.

Suffocating, draining, unbearable: that's how it feels with emotional amputation of the rabble.  .

You adapted at their lower level and lost your logic a little, now it hurts like all change ya know.  .

It's is so psychologically abusive to be gaslit or falsely accused it IS the dark night of the soul kids.

## NARCISSISTIC SIBLING ABUSE IS REAL

Narcissistic sibling abuse in childhood runs deep to our core and even later as adults we're sore.

In going dense about what I knew--deliberately for your approval--I became crazier than you.

You knew the truth but lacked boldness to state it. So it welled up and you were a fool, face it.

All those years I went mute and held it in. Now I'm writing it all out and you're the crazy one.

I want to thank you sisters and mom for my spiritual explosion as a result of this total bedlam.

Cuz you girls had me in such a vice grip there was nowhere to turn but God, thank you slobs.

Women are crueler than men cuz they think/chat all day about how to do them in/put it into play.

# SEASON OF TREASON

While I was studying and writing all day in my room they were gossiping and planning my doom.

I had no idea until years later what all those secret meetings were about, the collusion/slanderin'.

The victim doesn't know about psychology, he just senses **SECRECY** and it alienates him surely.

But if he boldly states his fears to the attorney or psychiatrist he's called paranoid, see sis?

## SOCIAL RATTLESNAKE IN YOUR CAGE

He had a pet snake who finally squeezed/killed him. She had a fake mate she was finally full of.

The social prostitute is so incredibly boring. Mr. and Mrs. Social Charm are superficial darling.

Above all, have gratitude for the narrow escapes God provided you, only recently revealed too.

Why this family division and curse? Because smears work with relationship-ruining narcs sir.

The electric release of energy being in an environment where it's safe to unfold and to be bold.

After all that I'd get combative in nothing flat. Mean, nice, it didn't matter I was just mad.

To the degree I held all that in, and for how long, I was exploding now, a rage-aholic it's called.

## ENERGY DRAIN OF SELF-DEFENSE

I have exuberant health now I don't have to defend myself against constant misjudgement.

# SEASON OF TREASON

You probably only remember 10% of the close calls/narrow escapes you made/God saved.

The saints have a stinging conscience, that's why you feel like this not cuza anything you did.

The clearer we get the grosser past sins look. Don't worry about that or let it be a hook.

As we clarify we're shocked at what we saw as mundaneity but rocked our senses surely.

When Jesus erases the past that puts your foes in contrast and God turns on them at last.

He uses your foes to punish you but when you repent now He turns his wrath on all those too.

Life is a ladder. At the bottom was clutter and torture but at the top is protection, success, closure.

## NO CLOSURE JUST PROSPER

Not closure cuz they're dead or in a rest home but having climbed the latter you're so much better.

Wuthering Heights: Start as a chump stable boy looked down on, end as a landowner gentlemen.

The female lowmind jezebels will interpret boundaries as rejection and even get violent about it man.

Rather than having PTSD/intrusive memories why not use and understand the latter analogy?

Implicit in the latter analogy is forgiveness. Otherwise there's a grudge, you're stuck in the past.

Your drinking etc. attracted lower companions who robbed you. It's a machine, the human zoo.

Rather than a grudge against the robbers see it as the very predictable evils of human nature.

Now as whole you wouldn't even let em in. You're well boundaried and there's no more bedlam.

Sin causes shame and in shame you're easily controlled as the hedge is down: no divine protection.

After separation from a toxic family it may be dark, isolating and lonely but becomes refreshing.

## ABUSE:  DARK NIGHT OF THE SOUL

With toxic abuse you're liable to experience the Dark Night of the Soul, a trashing of all you know.

You want nothingness after dross and clutter is dissolved to reveal the pure stone of all you are.

All the projections, introjections and blames laid on you are dissolved, now it's just the True Self.

You held it in abused all those years but now you're telling the world with a prosperous future.

It hurts like hell to face the facts but it explodes the past open to cosmic consciousness at last.

Your ego must die for your soul to thrive--that's why this part of the process hurts so much, aye.

A terrifying conflict: fall back to the dark comfort of past deception or go forward into the light son.

## I WAS A FOOLISH SYCOPHANT

I didn't wanna be a foolish sycophant child again but becoming who I am brought instant bedlam.

# SEASON OF TREASON

My Dark Night taught me valuable lessons of discernment and how to relieve depression.

"You are an humiliation and eyesore to our entire family" said the narcissist and her flying monkeys.

In a beautiful house I don't wanna be surrounded by old appliances & unfinished projects, ouch.

Get rid of all the clutter/crap/pork all around and you have yourself an estate free of bad fate.

The greatest attitude adjustment [AA] is Jesus not pot. I used to think not til' tar blocked thought.

## JESUS CLEARED UP THE WHOLE MESS

"I coulda gone to jail or locked up for life" said the grateful ex-drunk escaping all strife.

Jesus was persecuted, tortured & killed by mob of false accusers. Nothing is more apt than that sir.

Jesus answer was to REPENT. That gets rid of all your unwanted, uninvited guests in a minute.

The attitude adjustment needed is Jesus not pot. I used to think not til' all I did was cough & cough.

Jesus was falsely accused and killed by those in power. He was the anti-establishment in that hour.

Jesus understands all the sins of mankind. Jesus knows me like none other and He is so kind.

## IT'S JUST A CHICKEN COOP

See it this way: It was like a chicken coop as they were all buzzing about you as they chewed.

# SEASON OF TREASON

They have such a grudge from jealousy they simply won't let you up like a group or thugs.

JEALOUSY was a main reason for witchburnings. That's the human element doing it's evil thing.

Until that one fine day you move. You simply pluck yourself outa the matrix and instantly improve.

Now they have no one to talk about. Now you either become a legend or they forget your bouts.

It's like a chicken coop all buzzing about you until you go away then they forget you immediately.

## JEZEBEL AND FEMALE TRAITORS

I couldn't stand her. Though wonderful before she went off to college she came back a dam witch.

I couldn't stand her. Though cute as a kid she became radical and weird: disloyal/gossiper/traitor.

She'd trash my identity to anyone who'd listen, even with me in the room--this spurred me on.

She'd say horrible, outlandish things in her Karen smear campaign to family, neighbors or friends.

I was so horrified by the things she was saying about me I wanted to die. Words have power, aye.

Identity was so important I decided I'd do anything to disprove the bitch: she made me rich.

Perhaps you weren't the victim of Jezebel, why would she hurt her own kids? But maybe she did...

## IDENTITY & FATAL MENTAL ILLNESS

# SEASON OF TREASON

Because I lacked the tools to negate this identity struggle I succumbed to it instead and fell.

I became what she said I was: her accusations became my script which I acted out for years.

People get physically or mentally ill. I had a mental illness--screwed up in the head--then it left.

It was a **FATAL** mental illness. Screwed up in the head I coulda been dead but God saved me instead.

I had a Fatal Mental Illness but thank God I overcame it and most of its characteristics.

Children don't have the tools nor awareness to block these identity traps laid by the jealous.

On Sunday the Day of Rest you should stop work and **REVIEW** what you've done last week.

Call em "evil helpers" cuz it all starts that way but ends up more trouble than they're worth ok.

Things blossom when they blossom, stop pressuring me hon'. We'll know **THE END** when it comes.

It's hard as memories come up from your denial, the only way you could deal with your ordeal.

Although two died and one is in a rest home I can still feel the effects of the Cinderella Syndrome.

**INTROVERTS, UNITE!**

I said I'm not interested cuz I'm **NOT**. It's nothing against you mate, it just must be God.

You're angry I'm not interested? Something I cannot help, an inner power which is irresistable?

# SEASON OF TREASON

Don't invite me cuz I'm not social. My life is in my home and I don't like adapting to other people.

Don't invite me cuz I'm not an extrovert like you. I'm an introvert with a proud right to solitude.

It wasn't to lose weight, as in vanity. It was a Fatal Mental Disorder that was a real bummer.

Am I interested? If you could stay like this I would be but I've witnessed your wild variability.

## ANGELS AVOID ALCOHOL

Alcohol is likely to have an aggressive effect on anyone with immune problems. Lunacy/DEMONS.

The more sensitive the soul/body the more crazy the effect of alcohol so watch out honey.

If you need solitude gotta demand it not mal-adapt to others with alcohol, a social lubricant.

I mal-adapted to invaders [drip dry hangers] by getting drunk with em & ended up the worst of em.

I just gotta say I'm scared of alcohol today. It should be banned & put cannabis everywhere I say.

He didn't "become alcoholic", he resumed his drinking career from long before I knew the lunatic.

Cure for anorexia/bulimia is one satisfying meal a day but you're banned from groups if you say it.

## SEASON OF TREASON

Holy Spirit: These toxic memories of when I had no boundaries are killing me cuz it's PTSD.

# SEASON OF TREASON

You got what you gave. You were invaded by nuts cuz you misbehaved and they did God's work ok?

Don't tell me who I should be afraid of and who not. This is dangerous cuz my gut tells me what is what.

He is whatever he needs to be at any moment and he thinks whatever's good for him the lughead.

Collapse the bad past into one thing: you had a demon in you and with such a huge destiny a bigger one.

Bigger destiny, bigger demon that's all. You had more to overcome, learn/see thru it all, now walk tall.

How does an inferior man get his hooks into a superior lady? By demeaning and calling her shady.

I have little to complain about see. I didn't go thru the depression/world war just you imposing on me.

## COLLECTIVE NARCISSISM

Grandiosity, a sense of entitlement, vindictiveness: we see a rising tide of narcissism and it's a mess.

Collective narcissism fast becomes collective psychopathy with violence, defiance, contumacy.

Narcissistic abuse: attempt to leverage asymmetric power negating my separate/autonomous identity.

A narcissist spouse will accumulate power over you. He will isolate you from friends, family, pets too.

He'll take over your finances, employ you but restrict other income, take over your children.

He's always working to create a power asymmetry with you chained up and him with the gains on top.

# SEASON OF TREASON

He will use this power asymmetry to deny your separate existence and get everyone to agree to it.

Your separate existence--your self-efficacious agency--is what he aims to destroy to make you puny.

The narcissist wants you as a zombified extension of himself, not a glorious unit shining as a self.

He seeks to remove your personal autonomy--your IDENTITY--like any concentration camp see.

## HE HATES YOUR AUTONOMY

He gaslights you so you doubt your judgement of reality and this is a constant thing, in-fighting.

The fading ability to judge your own reality impacts one's memories, another decline in personal facility.

When you can't formulate coherent memories your identity is impacted and worsens daily.

Narcissistic abuse is using asymmetric power to counter, negate, vitiate and destroy another's identity.

Contumacy means they rebel against legitimate, logical rules you've laid out and may even lash out.

They hate you for curbing them, for asking for a little quiet or order or for saying "NO" over and over.

I woulda said NO, NO, NO, NO if I weren't so scared they'd hit me or other things from hell below.

You can't constraint a wild crowd. Restraints only incite more violence and defiant contumacy so loud.

I was so boundary-poor it was like a tidal wave as they only wanted more, that's the herd I abhor.

# SEASON OF TREASON

It's been years:  they're either senile or passed and no one remembers when you were such an ass.

You'll be saying "I learned so much from this experience with a narcissist it was even worth it."

## SMEAR CAMPAIGN

After quitting the narcissist he starts a smear campaign by putting himself self up and you to shame.

He may even show remorse and guilt promising change or counseling but it's a trick/not true of course.

Narcissism is a spirit which discards then hoovers you back in. Don't go back like your life depends.

You can bring God's disfavor from bad associations just as easily as sin. They ARE your sin friend.

Replace thoughts so they dissipate: They attacked me then but now I'm behind fence with locked gate.

Abuse cycle: idealize [love bomb], devalue [belittle], discard [reject], hoover [makeup/apologize].

Narcissists are parasites needing a host to feed them. If you're gone they'll just get new supply hon'.

After recovering from the terrible trauma of adapting to a narcissist you will feel like a million after this.

For he doesn't care about anyone but himself and only wants supply for which he'll use you up.

You can't protect a lie [that your government cares about you] without censoring the truth. David Icke

Their narrative is insane, impossible to stand on the evidence--with lies/deceptions they strangle us.

# SEASON OF TREASON

I had a cadre of hangers on that I couldn't get rid of until I learned to say "I don't want anyone around".

When she started to become what others wanted her to be she became a caricature, a mere wanna be.

## NON-COMPROMISING IS SEXY

The right attitude is not belligerent but it is non-compromising, even in a lady's voice said sweetly.

Most can be oblivious to everything around them but an empath cannot and thus the drugs come out.

If someone takes over your emotional life it can be the end of your life with vacillation and strife.

If someone takes over your emotional life it's the end of it with nightmarish vacillation and strife.

PTSD: The more toxic thoughts the deeper the neuropathways increasing anxiety, then repeat.

Only by the acceptance of millions was Janis Joplin ok but if one didn't he could destroy her in a minute.

Society is so pressurized that we can't live in it without guarding ourselves against it. John Lennon

It makes narcs insane that you have standards which if you stay with him are soon gone afterwards.

The silent treatment, violence or being discarded are possible outcomes of objecting to his darkness.

When she started drawing lines with her time and money she was discarded immediately, see?

When she laid out no-interruption office hours she was treated as an imbecile, traitor, a dirty whore.

# SEASON OF TREASON

Having boundaries was the biggest sin. I have so many I was violently targeted and harassed by him.

They're always shit-testing you for control but saying NO makes em run for the hills ya' know.

## DRAWING LINES MAKES EM MAD

When you draw lines in the sand you'll feel their wrath and frustration, it's called narcissistic rage son.

All-important boundaries make toxic people run for the hills but the well-adjusted accept them still.

An honest tip: whether men or women, nothing is sexier than the word "NO" cuz it makes em teachable.

Be like the joys of retirement: of letting it all go now and forgetting everything behind--I mean ALL.

His worst nightmare is being exposed so when you do expect a giant smear campaign imposed.

The first thing narcs do when you go no-contact is to act as tho' THEY went no contact, imagine that.

When she goes no-contact the narcissist must convince everyone else she's the one who's mad.

With your rejection he portrays himself as the victim and smears your reputation--it's a MUST for him.

PTSD is Satan controlling your mind thru bad memories. You should forget em but you can't, see.

God said "can't you just enjoy the beautiful world I put you in and ignore--or retire from--the filthy sinners?"

Can't you just put on retirement like cozy pajamas and let the immature past disperse into nothingness?

# SEASON OF TREASON

The therapeutic answer is eternity. In eternity there's no one but you and God: without people we're free.

## THE DECISION TO QUIT

You've decided to get the hell out. Don't panic or fight back just PRAY knowing God'll take care of it.

KNOW there's a very good reason you want out. Trust that, no more words and no more ouch.

You're outa the panic, humiliation, anger--you've DECIDED. Now just move into enlightenment.

It seems impossible cuza what y'all have together but it's NOT--with God He'll work everything out.

## CHEATERS ARE OUT

If he's a cheater, a pedophile, a whoremonger or pornhog you deserve to be OUT--AWAY from this, NOW.

NO MORE WORDS. When you've decided to get the hell out no matter what now start a fast quick.

I don't care if you have property together, if there's cheating in a partner you gotta get out dear.

THIS is why you cry all the time, it's finally come out--your GUT knows everything about that nut.

Be excited about your new life. You've DECIDED, you've started a fast and got a Christian counselor.

If everything's as you think it is, it's BAD. Stop denying the truth and see the patterns of that cad.

You've decided, fasted and contacted pastor for a Christian counselor now just SAIL ON OUT.

# SEASON OF TREASON

You feel so much better, having decided. It was the denial coming up to it that made you quite mad.

Now don't go back and stop arguing points you've made a thousand times, it's over/God says "She's Mine".

If there's a good reason for this, and there is, then God agrees--once realizing that it's a breeze.

**SUDDEN DEFLATION**

You were flying high creative and happy and suddenly he shot you down again albeit inadvertently.

So his symptoms morphed into something more socially acceptable--so what, he's still trouble.

God, help me get rid of this devil in my life. It's an old story but I'm vulnerable, give me Your advice.

It's just HIM. You know he's a faker and tho' he gets along as a joker suddenly you're down in the gutter.

Please don't constrain/rope me in thru financial dependency I need to be independently wealthy.

For I hate this, and there are false ties/old dependencies that are anachronisms and dysynchronies.

This current upset may be the very thing you've been praying for. God knows/reveals all ya' know.

Above all, be careful. Know who you're dealing with--stop one-upping and look forward to new life hon'.

If you are godly/repentant and you want this, you can rest assured God wants this and you're free sis.

Pray for escape. Now stay alert and fast for the hunch cuz God wants whats best for His bunch.

# SEASON OF TREASON

The answer to your urgent prayer was God's revelation about the bum in your nightmares, unawares.

Is your marriage a tight union or a leaky boat? Is he more interested in the neighbors or your mug?

Be wise--don't let em know what you're planning or thinking. Put NO cards on the table smarty.

I went thru all this so i could write this shit. I'm mad, I'm real mad the Daddy of Soul James Brown said.

## YOU FLUSHED EM OUT

By acting out your True Self it flushed her out and tho' it hurts now, count yourself lucky/stay calm.

It's not that I trusted you again, I just went back into denial. That was all, it's an illness mental.

You hate her guts, you hate his guts, you see it all, you're getting out--BE WISE, don't tell the nuts.

If you're anxious, confused, heart palpitating, terrified--trust these instincts: that somethin' stinks!

## STRESSFUL LIVING WITH THE DEVIL

The tension is unbelievable when you're living with the devil though he puts on a show all-aglow.

The false piety is unbelievable: "I'm filled with joy, love, gratitude, thankfulness and compassion."

She wails: I've turned from bitterness, worry, regret, anxiety, selfishness" tho' she's an angry witch.

I'd tell you what he did but you wouldn't believe me anyway so no wasted time, choose sublime.

# SEASON OF TREASON

The lady said "Ok I'm an angry bitch but I've a RIGHT to be fucking angry and no one can stop me".

BE WISE: don't let the enemy know secret plans so neat then move as God directs my sweet.

You don't want a leaky boat with neighbors knowing all your personal business but that's socialist.

You see what a pig he is, how he'll do anything for attention. Wait for the cue/don't yell at him.

Don't let him know what you think of him--a little man, a weasel, an immature human, the forsaken.

He hurt you and he must pay. There's a compensation for all acts good or bad and this is an old story.

## WORLD OF NARCISSISTS AND FREAKS

As long as we're in the world we're living amongst narcissists and freaks so fence up my sweet.

I'm so sorry this happened to you, again and again...and again. But isn't this becoming a pattern?

I'm praying for the WAY OUT while maintaining the pad for the pets cuz it's their niche/environment.

No need to yell and scream your points, it's all repetition anyway. trust your instincts and calmly say.

He couldn't rise to the task. He just couldn't keep up so got distracted on that level with rabble fuss.

Everything here is crucial for the love addict/trauma bonded to know as they escape hell below.

Ever since WWII narcissism has crept into the cultural consciousness and WE ARE IT where we sit.

# SEASON OF TREASON

Narcissism is a natural reaction to attack/negligence as we learn in life that no one cares for us.

Energy comes into self for protection, guarding, comparing, one-upping, doing the rejecting.

I don't wanna talk anymore, it's boring hearing your hammering so please give me office hours.

Tho' we lived separately I assumed we're on the same level but we were not, he's a lowminded devil.

The lady said "I have an ache in my gut and a swamp in my mind" and that describes life with a nut.

The left only wants free speech for those using it to trash America.

We live in a world where common sense is seen as wrong, outmoded, irrelevant, bad or mad.

Now is the time for all good men to come forward and pray for our country and this tragedy.

The youth are captivated by socialism/communism.  They have no idea of the deaths/misery from them.

Christian restraint is regarded as extreme when really it's just normal, righteous, happy and decent.

**BIDEN'S BAD. WE'RE BRANDON MAD**

Biden: "I'm going to appoint a black woman" means: not chosen on her merits but on her skin.

Supremes: Decent Americans always hated segregation cuz it dehuminized us--well so does this.

EQUITY means the most aggressive hostile form of persecution and prejudice imagined.

# SEASON OF TREASON

EQUITY means chopping off legs to fit an iron bed: Procrustean conformity called "diversity".

What about all her vast achievements? They're irrelevant, all that matters is her pigment.

A supreme court justice is supposed to represent the constitution not a race in the United States

Choosing the head judge based on race or gender is not only illegal/liberal it's dangerous as hell.

Bidenists: We want a America first judge and constitutionalist not a hard left woke activist.

Putin doesn't fear Joe one bit. Why worry a weak leader who won't secure his own border? He's a twit.

He was incredibly pragmatic and self-serving. Caution: that's the kind who will do anything.

## BIDEN'S PREJUDICE AGAINST US

Pres. Biden wants to send IRS to surveil your bank acct while giving your money to lawbreakers.

Joe Biden's an empty suit front man for [Obama wanting reparations] a time such as this: bam!

They've targeted our constitution for destruction and in its place will be a banana republic soon.

Russia wants nothing to do with our wokification and instead wants it's rich religious traditions.

While American conservatives fight a civil war Putin fears invasion of ideas of us foreigners.

Western wokism is Marxism, pure and simple. For Hollywood and elites it's the main principle.

# SEASON OF TREASON

These Wokists are no different than Bolshevik Marxists who wreaked havoc on Russia in 1917.

Marxists essentially believe ALL disparities are from discrimination and it's wrecking our nation.

Woke see all disparity--economic, education, whatever--is by definition intentional discrimination.

## IT'S ALL MARXIAN TACTICS

Marxists use a million ways to awaken society to how some are given much and some little see.

For Americans & Russia this is nothing new. The same thing happened to us in 1917 too. Putin

The Bolsheviks were absolutely intolerant of different opinions from their own. Vladimir Putin

What has this brought America to? Reverse discrimination and cancel culture/suits.

Western paralysis comes from the aggressive blotting out of whole pages of their history. Putin

Western paralysis comes from affirmative action and the renunciation of tradition [mother/father].

Renouncing the distinction between sexes is a milestone, a total renewal of society. Vladimir Putin

## RESENTMENT POLITICS

It leads to RESENTMENT POLITICS where a segment of society is seen as a permanent adversary.

Resentment politics: Liberals don't wanna fight wars overseas but right here at home, get it?

# SEASON OF TREASON

Wokism happened in Russia with "newspeak" as this new consciousness destroyed their lives see.

Wokism is surely a crime against humanity all under the banner of progress. Vladimir Putin

We've always known the disdain and contempt liberals have for us but their "F-YOU" is exempt?

To the woke we're the odious masses ignorantly thinking we count, as learned in their classes.

Feeling like aliens in our own nations, rallies give us a chance to rediscover our country/citizens.

According to Christian tradition our new world is already realized & we feel that in the rallies.

Thank you Jesus, I'm back in paradise again. I repented of bad friends and other affections.

## DEATH OF CITIZENSHIP

The death of citizenship means there's no distinction and we can't object to mass illegal immigration.

Globalism by its very nature is hostile to borders. It wants a one size fits all NEW WORLD ORDER.

With no borders there are no nations. That is in fact the goal of globalism: the demise of all of em.

Without nations there can be no citizens. We're now of the world, cogs in the wheel/communism.

Citizenship is now eroding under the global elite who give more credence to invading cheats.

Globalism creates a sense of entitlement where foreigners demand the benefits of citizens.

# SEASON OF TREASON

650 million people wanting to come here would be insane not to do it now for the BIG cash cow.

With death of citizenship our own government is free to treat "illegals" better than their own.

Without the protections deemed to us by our citizenship, deadly consequences will follow it.

## SAVIOR OF AMERICA AND THE WEST

Donald Trump came at just the right time and he's gonna save this great country of yours and mine.

Giving Trump an "F" on climate change is actually giving him an "A" on it.

It's so powerful, how could someone not serve truth? Cuz they've been twisted and they're fallen too.

Antifa sees free speech as the lever of oppression deserving of violence without any question.

When fascism comes to America it will come under the guise of anti-fascism. Vacuous punditry proves it..

We have high ground cuz we're Christians with morals, they have low ground as anti-Christians/morons.

Cops are told to stand down by mayors and higher-ups but they wanna fight these commie thugs.

The circle of prohibitive speech gets wider and more violent.

Guess what snowflakes, out in the world you're gonna hear republican views; oh no, boo hoo.

The snowflake culture will hurt the left if they continue to coddle these pests. Snowflakes melt when you say "law and order"

Being under tyranny of low IQ people leads to mental illness--the opposite to joy, creativity and fullness.

# SEASON OF TREASON

## CONSERVATIVE MEANS DECENCY

Conservative means: Decency, decency, decency. Ben Shapiro

MTV's brewing race wars, targeting whites--even old people and mothers with children they fight.

Those naked women in central park are sick creeps. They just wanna push the envelope for the peeps.

Obama did more harm to the country than any foreign army, as his divisive policies hurt us badly.

Out of control crime-wave in America tied to progressive policies for which we need an enema.

The democrat attitude is: "we don't know how any of this works so we're not even going to try."

Cities are death traps due to limited resources.

They knew it was gonna flood three days before but decided not to tell to prevent a panic or a war?

Zombiosis has taken over the land, the bible talks about it. It's government dependency, I'm sure of it.

This was the biggest flood in history and totally the most responsive presidency. Greg Abbott

Men in dresses running around beating up the defenseless in a prayer meeting: the fascist Antifas.

Once you see how cruel they are shut it all down (go inside, working all times) despite low IQ clowns

## WOMEN HOLD WOMEN DOWN

Feminist women: Once they think you're down they hop on the fallen hero bandwagon/you're forsaken.

# SEASON OF TREASON

Biggest tip of the day: If you don't eat anything the hunger will go away.

It's beautiful and catchy, a new psychology.

There's only one thing he could do: write a worldchanger. But til that time he made no sense to peoplekind.

You say there's no danger--I don't believe that, people are dumb enough to like her.

They are appealing to the dumb and since they're the majority that's all we hear all around.

So you're done. Just wait now as completion on earth becomes a magnet to the planned success link.

Liberals are only generous with other people's money. I'm familiar with this and it was a moral tragedy.

## STRESS SHRINKS THE BRAIN

If stress causes brain to shrink no wonder I was treated like a moron in those decades learning these points.

The main thing is I'm DONE. Tho' there's always details, I've won.

LOCK UP this communist or we're dead, as the dumbed down public seems to love her instead!

Dems have been hijacked by open borders fringe. Thanks to puppets like AOC it's even more deranged.

How could any feminist be for open borders? It is natural for women to want safety for their others.

In dumbed down generations the mindless masses are easily swept up into hysteria over demagogues.

Obama captured cameras and dumbed down masses and AOC's doing it the same way, I'm dismayed.

# SEASON OF TREASON

It's the ideas of Karl Marx repackaged for youth who are unaware of history and the millions killed too.

**FEMINISTS LOVE MUSLIMS**

Women's movement/marches show anti-semitism (blatant) but love of Muslims while we're hated.

I fear Cortez cuz of her appeal to a big chunk of angry entitled Millennials who could swing us into hell.

Women's march: blatantly anti-Semitic, cruel. Hate Jews and love Muslims feminist paradox.

Thanks to general madness we're entering a period of mass hysteria as people worship demagogues.

Good Lord she's an extremist and radical--a cult of hate! Loves Palestine, hates Israel/ICE? I'm dismayed.

All these types are puppets--primed and groomed pretty boys/girls to lead us into the globalist curse.

**AOC A FOOLISH DISGRACE**

AOL CORTEZ:  I'm limiting internet so I won't see your face or hear your words, a foolish disgrace!

It's when the mad masses worship superficial images--looks, style, coolness-- rather than truth.

IRELAND:  Land of saints and scholars ends up squashed by  low IQ pops dumbed down in squalor.

Hix politix is a blood sport: Greatest devotees will cast you to the wind when you don't serve their needs.

Karma  is particularly cruel to those who WERE riding so high when having power and we died.

# SEASON OF TREASON

So now AOC Cortez--rabid socialist divider/hater--is totally cool cuz she does the boogie/breaks the rules.

The ex-vegan obligate carnivore was still slender but now have curves like at top of hips: female verve!

Commie Cortez: We only have 12 years to save earth so who cares about property rights or paying for it?

Is government cared about future there'd be honest conversations about immigration which there isn't.

## IMPULSIVE EMERGENCIES OF LEFTIES

It's always an emergency to justify their stuff. Always gotta be done right now and to hell with facts bud.

Since Cortez is a landslide change moving the Overton window she'll get complacent and do herself in.

What's it gonna do to the economy by making it so difficult for the highest earners? Curses

To Cortez, everything's "immoral" except for those things which are truly immoral: immature girl.

It doesn't matter what's really there--naked click-bate is what grabs your selection for an affair.

I sense he has vile attractions. There's something in him and I've a knowing about these predilections.

It's just click-bait but that's what you click on baby.

At this point of pure recidivism (repetition) just give him enough rope to hang himself and watch him.

It's click-bait, man--if it's naked you'll click on it. Doesn't matter if there's nothing there, dig it?

# SEASON OF TREASON

He has prurient interests and vile affections--tho' he swears off of it the spirit comes back (inveterate).

Lusting after other people in minds--which is pornography--is offensive to God, the vile won't win out.

## FINAL JUSTICE VIA MILITARY TRIBUNALS

Judges have been seated, death chambers have been prepared. These traitors will die/they never cared.

Democrats love killing babies--especially newborns. That makes em happy while good people mourn.

All we gotta do is pay for it. If we pay enough we can stop the end of the world. Alexandria O-Cortez

Alexandria O-Cortez loves Swedish socialism while this open border country goes down in flames.

If Freelee loves animals why doesn't she go after halal slaughter? Cuz she's a leftist, muslims are brothers.

Why unequal outcomes: who can be creatively productive if they're interrupted to pray five times a day?

I took in an elderly cat when her owner had died. My life opened up--what wisdom's in her eyes!

Donald Trump is a master at fooling the democrats. The dems have low IQ and are like gullible brats.

Trump uses wall to fool dems, pushing em to extremist leftist/socialist positions--mad and unhinged.

Democrats cheering baby murder: "due date, due date, due date": after labor baby meets  grisly fate.

WALL: Even more important things going on behind the scenes--like mass arrests of democrat fiends.

# SEASON OF TREASON

**BYE BYE NANCY PELOSI**

That's why Trump's so nice to Nancy--not only civility but he knows she's going to prison quite speedily!

Ask ANY vegan radical: WHAT ABOUT HALAL and he'll escape or go mute cuz he's allied with it all.

Strict security issues at airports but NOT at our border? Pelosi's been pushed into a mental disorder.

Given the laissez-faire atmosphere it was easy and lucrative to be a traitor it was just globalism/had a flair.

The nice lady said to her husband: "Stop making me compete with twenty year old porn stars", the end.

Never have federal drug programs had more money yet drugs are at their peak, like all gov depts stink.

Oldstyle: She keeps everyone in the home happy. Newstyle: She makes em all miserable, modern tragedy.

Whatever Trump does which is positive they scream the opposite.

Reason Freelee turned off comments: Because she's so high, kind and spiritual she's too good for us.

Blue collars leaving democrats in droves cuz they're FED UP with left's fascination with open borders.

The most thrilling meditation is flying into heaven and leaving the earth and all it's inhabitants behind.

It's immoral that billionaires exist when the others are poor. Communist Alexandria O-Cortez

The existence of a billionaire is immoral but killing babies is a human right. Liberal narrative 2019.

**PARTY OF DEATH**

# SEASON OF TREASON

The American Democrats are now the part of death: let the illegal aliens in and kill the children.

If you're used to privilege equality feels like oppression but if used to oppression it feels like a privilege.

Don't answer the question you're asked but the one you want to be asked. Politician's creed

AOC: She says it convincingly, she knows how to pivot and she does it all shamelessly.

Alexandria O-Cortez: She's not smart or educated but shrewd and she has good political chops.

If prospering and keeping your own property is immoral then stealing it is moral as a corrective: get this!

Stats on millennials show they're depressed, anxious, stressed and suicidal-- open to demagogues.

## FALLEN AMERICAN CHURCHES

The absolute proof that American churches have fallen: they made the likes of you/your spouse deacons!

People have become so cruel and debauched, for sensitive souls it's just too much/we're out to lunch.

I'm not even going to argue with you creepy Millennials anymore. You've hurt me enough/I deplore.

It is fascinating to see the family re-assemble around our new member, an elderly cat: "pepper".

Vegans won't speak against halal slaughter cuz the enemy of their enemy is their friend against the west.

It's unethical to refer to a woman as "female" and promiscuity is celebrated to be equal to males.

**IT'S ALL FAKE:  VICTIMIZATION CULTURE**

It's all fake: Claim victimization because you're Latina, woman or even better, poor. AOL CORTEZ

AOL Cortez is very aware of the left's biases and she's exploiting those biases like a true con artist.

Oppressed Female Ethnic Minority has greatly benefitted her and now she's milking it, a great poser.

Her speaking in broad generalities and short sentences indicates her belief she's educated but she's NOT.

AOC's self-confidence & looks makes the even less educated believe in the dangerous things she says.

**NEW WORLD RICH**

In this new world rich people are characterized as greedy and evil while the poor are good and oppressed.

In this worldview it is unethical NOT to steal from the evil rich to give to the good and oppressed poor.

The left prioritizes style over substance. She is charismatic--that's what it's all about: on the surface.

We on the right get excited by truth but those on the left are excited by the charismatic, lookers too.

The left elevates the charismatic instantaneously while with the right it takes time to trust earnestly.

The way to reduce white supremacy in America is to reduce the racism against whites in America.

I'm facing heaven with my back to everything else I've known--pure illusion and a sad way to learn it all.

# SEASON OF TREASON

Freelee vegan won't eat an animal that had to die but she'll abort her baby and would do it again, no lie.

"Don't judge people collectively"--I wouldn't if they would only stop acting collectively/voting for enemies.

**KNOW YOUR GENDER: ONE OF TWO**

Knowing one's gender and race tells you how they will vote 90% of the time showing they have no spine.

University millennials: They make up what you think/castigate you for it and there's no arguing with it.

People in crowds, mobs, systems, tribes can become completely irrational: contagious madness of y'all.

Millennial delusions: In great danger/threat to their lives from circumambient sexism, racism, etc-isms.

College bureaucrats unite with narcissistic students to elevate their status to top dog victim on campus.

I went from fruitarian to starchavore to low fat diet to Atkins to carnivore. Reverse between em: SOAR!

It used to be strength and accomplishment but now our strange culture venerates victims much.

Where is celebrated heroism of the past? Strength, achievement--all gone cuz victims are the high caste.

There's no way they're gonna give up their sacred rarified status of victim, blocking true education.

The university is super-tolerant of those traits which can get you stoned or killed elsewhere without a prayer.

Without strong professors to resist this insane undertow, the weaker ones buy into it and it speedily grows.

Poverty rates are due to difference in cultures. But liberals see it as structurally obstructive (white vultures).

**GRADUATE, MARRY, WORK: NO POVERTY**

73% are not poor if they: 1. graduate high school. 2. wait until marriage for children. 3. work at a job.

Disparate impact analysis: any differences are based on RACE bias but this is B.S.--it's behavior sis.

How can it be structural racism when blacks are 10x more truant while Asians wouldn't never think of that.

Asians: Minimal out of wedlock births, push kids to college, no truancy, minimal violence=different outcome.

Different behaviors equals different outcomes. It has nothing to do with structural racism.

Instead of encouraging self-help the bureaucracies grow everywhere-- increasing the obstruction.

Black kids kill each other 10 x the rate of whites but the Obama rule says you can't cut em down to size.

ALL their bureaucratic rules makes you blame whites--it's ALL the product of our racism and the like.

Create habits in kids to create self-control and ability to defer gratification and they'll habitually keep em.

Keep to the ideas that are BIG then don't dumb us down to the million of ideas that are small. Everett Piper

Get rid of the big laws giving you perfect liberty and thousands of little laws rush in to fill the vacuum.

We're an anti-science culture which has dumbed down everything to our feelings not facts, for sure.

# SEASON OF TREASON

A lot of naive kids get into veganism for the six packs and thigh gaps that Freelee freely markets.

Vegans are causing cruelty to cats and dogs--obligate carnivores--by making em eat fruits and vegetables.

## RESPECT UNNECESSARY FOR CRAZY

We are instructed to live in peace with all peoples but not to respect their ideologies so awful.

Every leftist position holds an internal inconsistency.

The only reason liberals are against the wall is because they know it works. More voters, more perks.

Know this: Mass low-skilled immigration from poverty cultures is a dangerous drain on our society.

The push for quotas is the destruction of meritocracy in America which will then be destroyed by China.

SJW push for quotas is the destruction of scientific meritocracy and even in physics girls are newbies.

## VIOLENCE NOT PREJUDICE

People are incarcerated massively because we're so violent not because the cops are out to get us.

The refusal to talk about behavior and to ascribe prejudice to unequal outcomes is the modern insanity.

Racial crime rates is the one thing explaining the disparities in the prison system but it's taboo to say it.

Culture's what matters--bourgeois habits like deferred gratification, self-control and public space (not littering).

The current view is that females/persons of color are in constant threat to their lives from racism/sexism.

# SEASON OF TREASON

Capitalism is decentralized: one glitch doesn't go far. Socialism is centralized: hellish with just one error.

"Deluxe floors" like living in an oil field--makes me wanna die but symptoms dissolve when I get away.

The sinner's in a fog: of self-reproach, disgust, fear of discovery, covering tracks and codependency.

## SINNERS ARE MENTALLY ILL

The sinner is literally mentally ill and the body's sick soon too. He's outa the groove as ruin ensues.

No matter how rich, educated or connected the sinner always brings himself down as God gives him up.

I walked around in a fog and everyone hated me. That's the state of sin we all have to face, a human tragedy.

Not until repentance could I think clearly/present myself legitimately--our sins are evident to everybody.

The higher your talents the more you're messed up with sin. The best saints were the worst sinners friend.

It's wonderful to know it's just me and God. Not the public, the tech guys or those who never call.

Be the top 10% not the bottom 90%. Settle your mind now work on body: eat only meat for 30 days.

Womankind has degenerated into total leftist weirdness : virtue signaling yet know nothing of politics

The democrat's infanticide push reveals their immorality and any dem you know is the same, really.

Democrats: the ending of life is to be celebrated.

# SEASON OF TREASON

A woman always knows something's up--there's a disattention that makes her check his history/phone.

## WOMEN KNOW IN OUR BONES

We women know! We know in our bones something's up! So of course we check their history you nut.

The Mormon lady said DON'T check what he watches--but I say No, you gotta know though it shocks.

When men view naked females online the wife knows: disattention/distraction of a no-good husband.

When men view naked females online the wife knows thru lost focus on her OR over-compensation, bro'.

I am first, great and different but does that mean the herd's ready for me? Best is trivialized/they love mediocrity.

Ok, we'll always be sinners but we're supposed to TRY/not succumb to it.

Either you're distracted or over-compensating and your WIFE KNOWS buddy, watch what you say.

The best is to be married living in two houses separated by an inner courtyard.

Democrats will tax you MORE to pay for people who don't have a right to be here in the first place.

Democrats are now the party of late-term abortion, high taxes, open borders and crime. Donald Trump

The more you're to be on the HIGHEST (carnivore) the more degraded your looks with the other.

One of these days AOC will fall in front of all of us--demons like this always bring themselves down.

When 99% of the crowd is drunk, gnarly, unattractive, bad haircuts, overweight and sloppy it's easy to be king.

# SEASON OF TREASON

Date long, marry slow and divorce fast because crazy doesn't show up for two years you know, at least.

**IGNORE IGNORANCE, PUNISH RUDENESS**

Ignore ignorance, reward brilliance and punish rudeness. George Bruno

She'll gossip against you when things get bad--that's how she keeps you in line (just the threat).

Are you pre-programmed or genetically disposed to bad decisions? It's like a curse, so work against em.

College has become a fake rite of passage and nothing but prolonged adolescence. George Bruno

Someone new can totally open you up to new worlds. Let it happen, doesn't have to be love, go girl.

Men just want tranquility and sex (peace at any price) but feminism triggers women to **PICK FIGHTS**.

Trump is supposed to be divisive--dividing the good from the evil--and the evil dems can't stand that.

Hair doesn't make a woman and a beard doesn't make a man--just be a lady or gentleman.

**SEPARATION BRINGS INDIVIDUATION.** Repeat that 100 times cuz it'll save your life from demons.

**SEPARATION** and you don't have to tell em why. That's why silence is golden--they'll think back and cry.

The more you separate the stronger you get. If you gotta stay alone for life to feel it, do it without regrets.

Spend this day separating. Forget "unite"--separate is what makes you great cuz it's not them mate.

# SEASON OF TREASON

However he seems, think the opposite. Recall our slogan "op-truth" to keep yourself in happiness.

Never trust superficial personnas or your passionate attractions. Think: OP-TRUTH and stay on vacation.

## NEVER STAY STUCK

Don't stay stuck to anyone and instead revel in your home. That's my space as the Ace, never to roam.

The lady said "I had never felt so unappreciated" as she disconnected then her life took off, unaffected.

Donald J. Trump: Savior of the nation and perhaps the west since he started the nationalists.

The lives of so many women were lost due to cultural decline. Being told to be a slut or eat like a swine.

Yeah, you were just a swipe away and I did it, hurray! I've come back to center and enjoying my day.

Their love affair with abortion/infanticide will literally kill the liberals. That's always how it works, in cycles.

The most horrible thing was not us breaking up but the way your sorry ass kept coming back for sex.

SEO companies will make promises but they won't give refunds. Gotta do the keywords yourself, hon'

Good Christian man said "I've had more ass than a toilet seat" then I unsubbed from the elite.

If you sell yourself people will be in awe then begin to see your foibles: a spirit of familiarity to avoid.

I love to hear the wind sounds coming thru the window or rain on a tin roof. No music then = that's cool.

# SEASON OF TREASON

The wind, the rain, the sounds--these are the ELEMENTS. I want a more ELEMENTAL reality sense.

**ELEMENTAL:  LISTEN TO THE WIND**

I'm listening to the wind at 3 a.m. with two cats and two dogs and we're in another reality with God.

The Elemental Reality puts me in mental cornucopia: Eternal visions of magic coincidences by Jah.

The bible says in the End Times there will be One World Religion and we've already got ChrisLam.

How can I be sure you love only me if you like all the beautiful women you see but that's just modernity.

Add the wind-chimes on the porch, the bright stars, thrilling creative ideas-- we're as high as a kite Sis.

It's ok if he deletes it cuz I just wanted him to read it anyway, heh heh--so good deleting head games.

Religion means **TO BE BOUND** and I can't stand that, I want to move with God and what He says.

I'm listening to the wind at 3 a.m. with two cats and two dogs and we're in another reality with God.

It's homicide not abortion.

Democrats are the worst hypocrites: it's all about **HIX POLITIX**-- mucho money from the globalists.

Pornography is **CHEATING**. Repeat after me 1000 x then nip it in the bud to be happy, prosperous and free.

How sad: The more he says he loves me, due to over-compensation the more I know he's into pornography.

# SEASON OF TREASON

When there's lying you can FEEL IT. The most important instruction to spouses is to TRUST YOUR GUT.

**BETRAYAL TRAUMA IS DEEP**

Betrayal trauma: Like a broken plate glued back together, it'll never be the same/hard to trust sir.

He tries to say porn isn't cheating, that you're making too much of this, shifting blame: GASLIGHTING.

Marriage is SEXUAL EXCLUSIVITY and pornography is cheating--repeat after me 1000x or joy is fleeting.

How can I be sure you love only me if you like all the beautiful women you see in all your pornography?

He looks at 16 year old nudes and compares em to you--what are you, 40, 50, 60?--think of how rude.

Think of betrayal of spouse--sexual exclusivity bond--putting nudes on his heart when you're not around.

Men with low restraint—vs. conscientiousness--are snagged by cyber-nudes and lose everything dudes.

A conscientious person says "NO" and can delay gratification, a loser cannot--he gives in to sensation.

Your friends who hated him saw the devil instantly but you did not--so you had to learn the lesson freely.

The utter terror of BETRAYAL TRAUMA is something one never forgets. Like a bombed city by sadists.

I trusted him utterly so when I found he was least trustworthy my reality shattered/felt so unworthy.

Suddenly seeing you can't trust someone you trusted is the ontologically fatal insight: your world is busted.

HUMAN CYCLES. All of life is about the inversion of systems. Your time will come if you faint not!

# SEASON OF TREASON

Be like dogs and cats: Getting the upper hand when size has nothing to do with the Big Payback.

Day of Discovery: It's tough when you've been lied to and betrayed. It's hard to go on in utter dismay.

## SICKLY CYCLICITY

It's the sick cycles of going back into trust only to be betrayed, over and again. More isolation, no friends.

Upon PORN discovery he starts to gaslight (make you look insane) and trivialize (this ain't no big thing).

It's a rough ride when you don't know if you can trust this person now or in the future: constant black cloud.

It's rough when your hopes and dreams have been shattered--you're unsure how to come back together.

## BETRAYAL TRAUMA

How quickly betrayal trauma can turn into alcoholism so please be careful in your reactions to his sins.

Betrayal trauma matters. She's not just mad at him, her entire world and reality has been shattered.

Betrayal trauma: The thing about trust is when it's gone, it's gone. I depended on you/I want my momma...

You pull the rug out from under me and expect me just to forget it as you trivialize it as a sin/repeat it.

Most therapists don't want to work with a betrayed spouse cuz they're boundariless, difficult, full of rage

Her angry outbursts make sense if you put a betrayal trauma frame around it--locked in/can't help it.

He says it's over, she finds something the next week: that's called Staggered Disclosure and it's a bitch.

# SEASON OF TREASON

**Betrayal Bonds: Having been isolated by the folie a deux the partner uses the abuser as her consoler.**

**Words are cheap with creeps.**

**The more he says he loves you the more you know something's up. Over-compensation is a button.**

**Contradictions are the symbol of addictions. "I love my wife" but then he's snagged again, bad decisions.**

**The Day of Discovery of your husband's pornography addiction brings anger, hopelessness, betrayal.**

**RISKING MARRIAGE FOR A NUDE PIC**

**He gambled away his whole marriage just to see nude teens.  That's blindness from hypofrontality it seems.**

**Oh the darkened minds of men escaping into sin then working to deceive so she'll stop bugging him.**

**Secondary trauma comes from religious leaders insisting she forgive (so soon) after discovering his porn.**

**Going thru history/wallet: Full Disclosure was necessary to see if she can trust him or not--she cannot.**

**He not only breached expectations of sexual exclusivity but also core Christian values that makes us happy.**

**Results of pornography: Broken families, loose relationships, malleable minds and shattered societies.**

**Using pornography repeatedly literally erodes our will power and moral compass: society won't last.**

**With hypofrontality the brain actually reads urgent warnings as urgent desires and thus the lost morals.**

**Conscientiousness is control of impulses/desires while delaying gratification. Porn wrecks this son.**

# SEASON OF TREASON

Just like that, he'll be gone with the wind. You prayed to your Rescuer, your Savior God, and He listened.

Keep envisioning when the devil will be gone from your midst. That's been the whole obstruction, the gist.

He/she/they held you down from the very beginning. Wolves in sheep's clothing, frenemies.

Make a list of all friends/family who hated him from the beginning. Then to please you they let him in.

Since with time you became isolated with just him, betrayal trauma shattered you to your core, friend.

## ISOLATION INCREASES SHATTERING

People minimize Betrayal Trauma when it is a most serious and painful deep fissure: a reality-buster.

Suddenly seeing reality is NOT what you thought it was, and it's so blatantly true--undeniably now too.

He was snagged by nudes JUST LIKE he didn't clean his room. Disorderly too, and poorly groomed.

Never stop talking of Betrayal Trauma occurring across the world: husbands gawking at young girls.

Don't minimize what he's done, he must eat crow. He turned your world upside down but now you know.

Pour it out, you're not weak to express your outrage and hurt. This is a terrible betrayal by that jerk.

Pour it out, I know how you feel. My gut roared in pain for weeks after my discovery about that heel.

Don't worry, now that you know you'll be calling all the shots from no on. Your problem was denial, hon'

# SEASON OF TREASON

I will never stop telling women to take betrayal trauma seriously and what it means--shattered dreams.

Don't worry the devil will be dead or gone with the wind, one way or the other you're able to breathe again.

Pornography has degraded females as a supernormal surplus has devalued women in men's eyes.

If he has an endless plethora of desirable women online it distorts his perception of his kind.

If you don't look like perfect porn stars you're devalued on the sexual market--good Lord think of that.

## PORN OBSCURES PERCEPTION OF FEMALES

Don't worry God'll get rid of this mentally ill dude for you.

New correlation: as women become manly men move into porn mainly.

Pornography obscures his perception of females so he's not satisfied with the loyal women in his life.

Not just porn, he's been watching "perfect females" in movies for years, studying them girls.

Rather than talking in bed with you he chooses to be watching a movie with that girl he's studying.

Before a doctor's visit or church he'll bring a big box of donuts so they attend to creeps: attention he seeks.

Pornography cheapens women when they're the most important part of society creating/raising men.

You oppress her long enough--with your porn and lying--and eventually she's tough/no more crying.

Changes in her perceptions of reality and especially SELF-concept. Instantly she's obsolete, dull, inept.

# SEASON OF TREASON

The **NEW** Marxism is Radical Social Justice. It's happening in South Africa-- pure racism and violence.

Social Justice is never equality of opportunity but of **OUTCOME**. It is dangerously Procrustean.

What's it gonna take for you to see what your friends saw in him at the beginning was the truth?

Cops can find it on your computer--you're going to jail. Your wife can find it too--that marriage will fail.

## ECLIPSING REALITY BY HIS INFIDELITY

Searching his constant infidelities took up my whole reality concretized in history then **NOT**, and I was free.

No fool like an old fool--they're as sick as they come. They were always evil yet veiled but with age, none.

True passion in death--who they really are shows up at the end. Foolish, pitiful, never ever your friend.

When the last Russian czars let Rasputin--pagan mystic--into their family it was the end, then the tragedy.

People let paganism in to solve their problem but then secondary problems sprout up always, amen.

Building a wall will violate the rights of millions of illegals. Nancy Pelosi

Rules of all old world leaderships: Orthodoxy, autocracy, nationality, the church, the leader and state.

Women tend to accept things that are wrong.

Those congresswomen in white were evil for hating President Trump and not applauding--it's appalling.

It's ok to break it off but you don't keep comin' back--not for that.

# SEASON OF TREASON

Porn vids line up on the right. He needs great self-restraint to not look at that for curiosity kills the cat.

I suffer, I write. That works for awhile and I'm alright. Then it builds up again, another nugget in sight.

Women: Instead of putting their foot down against porn, they get plastic surgery to compete with whores.

Undeniably, democrats are now the party of abortion, regardless of how barbaric the procedure is.

## BARBARIC LATE-TERM ABORTION (DEMS)

Barbaric late-term abortion will lift up the pro-life movement like it's never been lifted up before. Pres. Trump

Dem's morbid enthusiasm for prenatal infanticide is causing ordinary Americans to recoil in horror and cry.

Death warrants for full-term babies: The American people are letting them know, loudly and clearly.

Liberal fems actually go along with this crap, accept it, and even have porn collections of their own.

Where there's most porn (UTAH) there's most plastic surgery as women compete to be nasty.

Why do liberal women always dress in WHITE? It's FAKE GOOD like their narrative, a phony blight.

Women dressed in white were applauding louder for themselves then America's great accomplishments.

The lady said "I'm willing to shove it under the rug AGAIN for the sake of kids and peace at home".

It's such a privilege for women to be born in America today and yet white robed witches shout rape.

# SEASON OF TREASON

Feminists are all for women--except those raped by illegal immigrants or baby girls aborted: what fakes!

While ignoring anything Trump had to say, women wildly cheered themselves in full narcissistic display.

No greater contrast: between a mother holding her infant child and the recent displays for infanticide.

## SELF-ESTEEM OF OLDER WOMEN SMASHED

The nice lady said "My self-esteem went out the door, I couldn't compete with a 16-year old porn star."

Democrats demand to slaughter viable children. Party of crime: they support infanticide but no guns.

Dems can't go against killing babies fully formed cuz as it contradicts their arguments for abortion.

Just like democrats in slavery days--voting against seeing blacks with human rights deserving pay.

Democrats attack the most innocent of human beings with their bloodlust. Put em all in Gitmo--you must!

Sad that it took the most barbaric and inhumane policies to force moderates to distance themselves.

Abortion on demand is unapologetic infanticide.

The bible says in the latter days there will be demons running around en masse, many in our congress.

Infanticide: Why do we even need a law--that's blatantly illegal. Pres. Trump

He's not a pediatrician but an ORGAN HARVESTING DOCTOR. Learn to see through images, sir.

Please God help me to resist hating women who have become so dumb in their immature governing.

# SEASON OF TREASON

The people behind this know what they're doing--it's formulaic, unified of purpose, strategic/directed.

MAGA rallies and SOTU speeches: How very clever our guy is!

I'm with God, you guys can go to the devil. We see who you are now, a clear division/not on our level.

We're fighting devil worshippers and these entities want children not just the organs they're harvestin'.

## WOMEN SELF-CONTRATULATING DOING NOTHING

Women cheer in narcissistic self-congratulating--compared to the dignified men, how childish and boring.

Instead of applauding Hispanics' lowest unemployment EVER, women applauded themselves as clever.

Hey, you in the white--you've revealed how incredibly self-centered you are, an embarrassment not "stars".

Cortez "had a rare bad night, looking not spirited, warm and original as usual but sullen, teenaged, at a loss."

"Why should I be spirited/warm with that embarrassing SOTU--he offered NO plan or future vision". Cortez

## PSYCHOPATHS IN POLITICS

You absolute psychopaths. The fact you'd even discuss post-birth abortion is vile/we'll NEVER forget it.

Democrats are the party of murdering babies about to be born. Sweet little babies, burned and torn.

Cortez aligning with dems on false fronts: constitution butchers, vile as hell and ready for GITMO jail.

No one's telling women to smile and NO man is catcalling them! MGTOW don't even want em as friends.

Things didn't go her way. Trump hit it outa the park & shunned socialism and she was the embarrassment.

"We wish to UNITE our community" means they're new age non-Christian cuz Jesus said DIVIDE to be free.

The "Christian University" is so into justice warrior BS they see Shapiro as hateful, divisive, offensive.

Church sees Trump as two-timing philandering mendacious reality TV star while placating justice warriors.

It's not the whole church--80% real Christians with the truth, 20% upper elites no different from liberals.

## THE "UNITY" (FAKE) CHRISTIAN ELITE

The "unifying" Christian elite giving cum-bay-ya sermons: that's why we love Donald Trump our man.

We're so sick of the social justice thing when we see it in the Christian elite it's horrifying, bland, effete.

We're so sick of the unfair, asymetrical selective moral outrage, in fakes like Cortez smiling on a stage.

The politics of grievance dominating university/church elites is merely a new form of privilege/it stinks.

Liz Warren sought to become a beneficiary of the racial diversity program that SHE helped advocate!

When universities ban speakers they don't want em exposing their obnoxious elitist entitlements, ever.

Unsatisfied at having all of their needs met they make up these ridiculous causes to rant about.

Trump knows their stand is so outrageous they're gonna FORCE the point for moralists.

# SEASON OF TREASON

Nancy Pelosi has mastered the art of subtle contempt or maybe she just needs some more fixodent.

Green is the new red.

Whoever assists you with cyber stuff is chosen by God to attend to your work. Most don't care, the jerks.

Remember most don't care to not be hurt on the internet. They're entirely selfish/want your neck.

Feminists complain of rape but are ok with pornography--they aren't moralists, they just wanna bitch.

I hate democrats more than I can describe. The gutter evil, slaughtering baby people and so egotistical.

## ACHING GUT TELLS ALL

As I write Social Psych manual I have an ache in my gut recalling ugly system dynamics and what not.

This concludes Karen Kellock Klass for the day, it's depressing learning things about the race.

Is it not You, O God, who cast us off? And You who did not go out with our armies? Psalms 60: 10

Democrats are dependent on the female vote and are attuned to women's issues like to abort.

Due to concern for female fate America is sleepwalking into socialism not the values making it great.

## GREEN HEADACHES

Eat your greens using delicious dressings masking bitterness before the migraine headaches.

While recovering from nitrates in greens I had tomato sauce: more migraines from nightshades.

# SEASON OF TREASON

No one can believe greens are a poison. That's the damage the "green movement" has done.

Don't listen to any diet advice even mine. Just set your goals, see the truth and experiment--you'll be fine.

You see I have the spacescape on one website and the dayscape on the other: I thought it clever.

Anyone can learn a program like word press but can you write code for a designer not degrading it?

You've made it. Formula crystalized, the matrix defined, it's all beautifully filled in, **NOW ENTER IN.**